Disrupted

Disrupted

On Fighting Death

&

Keeping Faith

Julie Anderson Love

CASCADE *Books* • Eugene, Oregon

DISRUPTED
On Fighting Death & Keeping Faith

Cascade Books
An Imprint of Wipf and Stock Publishers
199 W. 8th Ave., Suite 3
Eugene, OR 97401
www.wipfandstock.com

ISBN 13: 978-1-61097-095-2

Cataloging-in-Publication data:

Love, Julie Anderson.

Disrupted : on fighting death & keeping faith / Julie Anderson Love.

xii + 166 p.; 21 cm—includes bibliographical references.

ISBN 13: 978-1-61097-095-2

1. Love, Julie Anderson. 2. Brain—Tumors—Patients—Biography. 2. Cancer—Religious Aspects—Christianity. I. Title.

BV4910.33 L7 2011

Manufactured in the USA.

For Greg

Contents

Acknowledgments

I MET a man recently who said he could write a book in two months. "Just write and never look back." The Lone Ranger of writers. The emergence of this memoir could not be more different. It is the result of so many people; their butt-kicking, loving, pushing, and pulling me along the way is what made it all happen. So thank you all. Mom—for all of the above; Pam—for believing all along the way; Heidi—for being my first real critic, who told me to keep it up; Catherine—for your wisdom when I most needed it. Terry—for serving as my first serious proofer.

And the kind, thoughtful, demanding instructors at University of San Francisco. You, who took on my project with all manner of seriousness. You cared enough to be honest with me and it made all the difference. Thank you.

Thank you all.

Preface

Anomalies

I SHOULD not be writing this. I had a malignant brain tumor. I had an extremely malignant brain tumor. By all medical statistics, I should be dead. Last time I checked, dead people don't write. My life is a protest against scientific reason. It is anomalous to biological data, a burr in the side of medical statistics. This story is a journey through the shadow valley. This is a story of betrayal and the devastation of a life. This is a story of facing impossible odds, asking absurd questions, laughing in the face of complete and utter disaster.

∞

For over two years I did not know if I would live or die. At twenty-nine years old, I discovered that I had a voraciously malignant brain tumor, a *pinealblastoma*. Because it is also the most rare of tumors, there is a dearth of statistics. And because it is so fast growing, and because it's not satisfied with its location in the brain—it sends out seeds throughout the brain and spinal cord—the statistics researchers do have are utterly, thoroughly grim. If you are on the hunt for any flicker of hope, do not go to the numbers.

And yet. And yet, given all of the bad news, the good news is that a few of us do make it through. Even science concedes nothing is ever 100 percent predictable.

Through brain surgery, over a year of monthly surgical chemo treatments, and finally radiation, I survived. Or was it through the prayers of my friends and family, along with the Buddhist meditations? Was it the laughter? The cards that stuffed my mailbox silly? Or was it because of all the friends who made it their business to join me in this journey? And then the meals, so many meals delivered at our door—the best way for a church to care for one of its own.

Or was it because I fought like crazy, perfecting the art of being the patient from hell? Could it be I'm here because I didn't let God off the hook, but took my complaints to this One who knew me through and through, and perfected the art of being the Christian from hell, if you'll pardon the term?

On second thought, don't pardon the term. When you face the likelihood of your imminent death, who else would you be?

This is a story of redemption.

1

≈≈

Stormy Waters

I WILL never know when it actually began. The symptoms were quiet, small, hardly worth attention. A serious illness can start with little warning—a slowly changing mole, or a tiny pebble buried deep in your breast. How do you know when to take a symptom seriously, or when to take an aspirin and go to bed? My attitude had always been to not overreact. My body was basically healthy—I'd never had a serious illness. With sleep and some Tylenol, most things resolved on their own.

My first position out of seminary, in 1990, was to be the associate pastor for a medium-sized Presbyterian Church in the small town of Albany, Oregon. My life was busy. I do remember seeing my doctor, Lynn Bentson, sometime in the summer of 1993. I was having trouble focusing on readings when I led worship—the lines of text would hover over one another. But in describing this to her, I said the text was blurry and hard to read. She wasn't worried and suggested I needed more protein. She told me to eat peanut butter before leading worship.

In the fall, I started losing energy and often came home in the afternoons for a nap. Mom was concerned. I simply thought it was because I worked hard. There were moments when a thought, a small voice, suggested my lack of energy was more than the result of overwork. But I had never been one to listen to small voices.

I grew up on a dead-end street on the Eastside of Seattle. Our street was packed with kids who played kick the can, hide and seek, and sardines most summer days. Our house was at the end of the street, which butted up against forty acres of field and forest. We chased one another down forest trails; we divided into teams, made forts, conducted fake battles.

One day we were taking turns jumping our bikes off of the hill that was the front yard of our neighbors across the street. "Hey, Julie!" Trevor called "Why don't you try my bike?"

I looked at his bike. The seat of it came up to my shoulders. A small voice suggested maybe this wasn't the best idea on the planet, but that voice was overruled by the other, louder voice in me, a voice conscious of a challenge: *You're not going to wimp out, are you?*

"O.K., I'll give it a shot!"

I jumped on the bike, was airborne before I knew it, and came crashing down to reality. Reality being the blacktop of our street. My chin broke my fall.

Suddenly, I was in the back seat of someone's car. My mom had a rag pressed to my chin as I sat in her lap. She held me and just once peeked under the rag, only to gasp and put it back, soggy and blood soaked. She bit her lip and turned to look out the window.

One thought instantly became my determined, six-year-old mantra: "I will not have stitches. I do not want stitches. I will not, do you hear me? NOT have stitches!" It was hard to say out loud with Mom holding so tightly to my chin, but I was determined to let everyone know the deal.

But ER docs don't listen to the rantings of a six-year-old, especially one who is covered in blood, her chin bone showing through a wide-open gash. Needless to say, I didn't win that battle. Still. I had a sense, even then, that my body was *my* body. I had every right to declare what would or would not be done to it.

In the fall of 1993, the small voices grew, fed by doubts that lingered on the edge of my days and refused to go away. One morning in early December, I came to work with a raging headache, but a young mom in our church had recently called the office and told us of a virus going around that caused nasty headaches. That gave me a fleeting sense of relief. A virus. That must explain it. Denial can be addictive—it made the fear go away, for a while anyway.

One Saturday that December, Pam, the church's office coordinator, stopped by our house.

I had first met Pam in August of 1990 in Chuck's office. Chuck was the senior pastor, and the church had made the decision to hire me as their new associate pastor the night before. Pam sat on a couch in the office, her bright pink-and-green floral dress outfit perfectly matching her earrings and pink lipstick. She sat, shoulders squared, paper and pen in hand, ready for whatever would come. Frankly, I had yet to meet someone who paid so close attention to every detail of self-presentation. *Note to self: this woman is way too in control. Stay under the radar. Avoid her at all costs. Just do your job and let her do hers.*

But then a single question changed everything between us. At our second staff meeting, Chuck and I were getting up to leave when Pam asked, "Do you think you'll have children? My daughter and I were talking last night, and she wondered about it. So, what do you think?"

What I thought was, who the heck are you to be asking me this kind of question my second week on the job?

What I thought was, Chuck is trying his best to get out of the room as fast as he can.

What I thought was, she's taking a gamble here, and I'm going to go for it.

"To be honest, I don't know . . ."

Given that Pam was fifteen years my senior, one would think ours was merely a working relationship. But one would be wrong. Though we were different in so many ways, we never ran out of things to talk about. The first fifteen minutes of each workday were spent catching up on the night before: what we made for dinner, the books we were reading, what we thought of the latest movie. Talking with her, there would be a distant echo in my heart. Glancing at her, searching her face, I wondered, *don't I know you from somewhere? Have we met before? Not just met, but have we known each other before?* How else could she feel so familiar, like a pair of old jeans? How else to explain the deep understanding we shared?

Pam stood in the doorway of our little house that December Saturday.

"You don't look good," Pam said. Her seriousness startled me. She didn't get concerned by much.

"I just took some Theraflu, I'll feel better in a moment." I explained, trying to sound casual and sure of myself. She nodded her head, unconvinced.

My head pounded; pain blinded me to much else. I leaned back on the couch, watching my husband Greg wrap the stocking stuffers that cluttered the floor.

"Call Dr. Bentson, Julie. I think you need to get this checked out," Pam said.

Dr. Bentson didn't seem overly worried. She was something of a nervous, chatty kind of bird. She had long, thick hair, a throwback from the sixties. And she talked. A lot. About anything. She talked, maybe thinking that was her way to connect with her patients. Or maybe it kept her from worrying about what might be before her? Or it could be that that's simply who she was, and her friends were all introverts who were grateful to have the airways filled with her chatter. She'd been my primary-care doc for two years, and I'd learned to steer her with appropriate questions. Her medical notes from that mid-December visit describe my problem as fatigue. Her notes suggest a mild sinus congestion, for which she prescribed an antibiotic.

A week later, Greg, and I went to Leavenworth, Washington, to cross-country ski and celebrate our anniversary. Leavenworth is a reinvented town. Nestled deep in the Cascade Mountains, this one-time logging community had gone bust, and by sheer determination became a little Bavarian village, with all things mountain-peaked and gingerbread facing.

I didn't feel great, but not horrible. I kept thinking it was just chronic sinus problems, or a determined virus. The second day out, we stumbled into some deep snow. We were trying to make it down the gentle slope; it wasn't going well and my ski kept popping off. Exhausted, and having absolutely no fun, I stopped and sobbed melodramatically, "I'm stuck! I can't move. Up or down. I'm stuck! What's going to happen to me?" It was a pathetic attempt at humor, whining and crying for help all in one. Greg didn't laugh, probably rolled his eyes, and continued slowly down, trusting that I would follow.

If I veer towards the impulsive, nonrational side of things, Greg is mostly my counterbalance. We met through a friend in common at Pacific Lutheran University when I was a freshman and he was a senior. Greg was blond, medium build, and almost daily wore bright yellow sweat bottoms (yellow and black are the colors for PLU). But what made him stand out, besides the yellow sweats, was the way he moved. Maybe it was just that he was perpetually late, but he always moved with great intention. Fast. He had somewhere to be, something important to do. He even walked to the library in a hurry, as if the thought of reading that textbook on modern European history was better than sex. He was on the crew team with his identical-twin brother, so was in great shape.

Frankly, it made no sense that we were attracted to each other. We had very little in common. He was a history major; I was utterly not interested in history. He was a thoughtful man who asked serious, threatening questions of his faith. Can God be trusted? Where is God when terrible things happen in your life? How can you read the Bible and take it seriously when it's a book that is culturally conditioned, full of contradictions and sexist declarations?

I was entirely sure of my faith, liked my Bible, and pretty much didn't have any questions.

When I was young I wanted to know about God. My parents weren't fanatical churchgoers; it was more of a week-to-week kind of thing, like mowing the lawn or washing the car. So it was up to me to motivate them to go. I loved Sunday school classes; I loved hearing stories about the people in the Old Testament.

I was often in the bathtub when I was young. Not a bathtub filled with water, but a dry one. When I was eight years old, I'd read this little book, *Hotline to Heaven*, which suggested getting in the tub to pray as no one bothers you when you're in the bath. The bathtub I used was in the kids' bathroom. It was surrounded by blue-purplish metallic wallpaper and had a long counter with two sinks that my brother, Steve, and I shared. The mirror had a wall of lights above it, happily showing any blemish, zit, or dark circle.

Hotline to Heaven explained that when you prayed, you were giving things to God, so you only needed to pray for something once. Thinking back on it now, even though it was a simple little book, I realize it was really a book about trust.

The amazing thing was, God and I had an incredible track record. One day, as I was just settling into the tub, Mom knocked on the door.

She stuck her head in. "Can you please pray for Uncle Glen to get a job? He's having trouble finding one, and he really needs it."

"Sure, no problem."

I don't remember how long he had been jobless, but it must've been a while.

Within a week, he landed a great job.

Trust came easy in those early days. I trusted my family to take care of me; I trusted the neighborhood kids to play with me. I trusted my mom to listen to the stories of my days, and trusted when she told me I was beautiful and smart that she meant it. I trusted God to hear my prayers and to act on them.

Greg and I attended a dialogue presented by three faculty members from the religion department at Pacific Lutheran University. It was a debate about the accuracy and relevance of the Bible. While the New Testament professor insisted that the latest translation, the Revised Standard Version, was extremely accurate in translating both the Greek and Hebrew, the professor of ethics dismissed that with a wave of her hand.

"What we need to be concerned with is not the word-for-word accuracy of our translation, but how the message of the New Testament, especially the Pauline letters, silences women and lifts up an oppressive, sacrificial love, that keeps women in their place. How can anyone call this 'good news'?"

"What I think is most transformative about the Bible is the notion that power is born from weakness," countered the professor of theology.

After the debate, Greg and I sat in my dorm room, carrying on our own debate for four hours. I actually had no problems with the Bible, and heatedly argued for its veracity and power. Greg pounded me with questions.

"What about the fact that there are two creation stories? How can you take them both literally?"

Good question. I'd never considered that before. "So what? What's the big deal about that? Maybe they are just saying the same thing with different words." Arguing was much more fun than agreeing. I loved the fact that this man sitting next to me took me seriously enough to debate.

Even though we were continents apart when it came to religious issues, we never seemed to run out of things to talk about. He came to find me every day that winter. Sometimes after a class, I'd find him outside the room. Another time, I walked one way across the quad, only to run into him as he ran to a meeting. We hiked together, went running together. We went to the University Center for dinner together. I often tried to convince him to go out for dinner, but his argument was that this food was already paid for, and it was good. Why should we go out?

When we began to date, a month after we'd met, he paid a visit to Ron Vignec, one of two campus pastors.

At the time, which would have been 1983, both campus pastors were named Ron, but that is where the similarity ended between them. They couldn't have been more different physically, personally, or spiritually. Ron Tolefson was the quintessential embodiment of "Lutheran Pastor," a perfect model for Garrison Keillor's imagination. He was slim, always wore grey slacks and a light grey shirt, and always wore the white clergy collar that symbolized his office. He looked like a model out of the pages of a catalogue for all things religious: stoles, robes, liturgical calendars, religious candles and small communion sets for visiting shut-ins. Even his hair was perfectly parted on the side and reminiscent of Glen Campbell.

And then there was Ron Pierre Vignec. He wore overalls that stretched over his vast belly, and flannel shirts that made him look like a logger who'd somehow lost his way. He walked around campus with a bow-legged gait and in Birkenstocks.

Vignec was unlike any pastor I had ever met. His hair was dark, thick, and wavy. He had a beard. Students nicknamed him Jerry Garcia.

It must have driven Ron of "all things Lutheran" crazy that as he did his best to play by the rules, perform the liturgy smoothly, and fulfill all of his many expected pastoral obligations, Vignec wandered around campus and hung out with the students. He talked with a Bronx accent about what it meant to be "'yuman." His office was crammed with books—on the shelves, on his desk, on the floor. He had weavings from South America on the walls. The fading poster over his couch depicted a church a sanctuary from the perspective of a pulpit. A few bored people sat scattered in the pews. In one of the pews, close to the front, sat Jesus, sound asleep.

In his idealistic youth Greg had made lists for his future life. One list detailed a perfect life partner. Among other things, he imagined his perfect wife would be the same age and one who held the same beliefs.

"How can this be?" Greg asked Ron. "She doesn't fit. Julie is not what I expected."

"She's a gift," Ron told him.

The winter of our eighth anniversary, a few days after our ski trip, we went to my parents' home just before Christmas. The next morning a pounding headache woke me up. I went downstairs, turned on the Christmas tree lights, cuddled up beneath a blanket, and prayed for relief.

"I think you need to see a neurosurgeon. This isn't right," Mom said when she found me there.

I was genuinely surprised. A brain surgeon? Even for Mom this seemed extreme. I laughed.

"A neurosurgeon? Don't you think that's just a little drastic?"

Frankly, I don't know when she became a worrier. Mom is incredibly bright. She can cook up a feast, kick your butt at Scrabble, run a law firm, win golf tournaments, skate around the Web, and listen until she drops to any story you want to tell her. But all the while, in the deep of the night, she will worry. With most things she will worry until she comes up with a solution. Which could be considered a good thing, as a solution frees her up. Except her ability to solve one problem only emboldens her to take on others.

But as her imagination is vast and active, worrying is just one of the things she does well. She not only worries; she shamelessly alters reality to her liking. She sees novels hidden in my small sermons; she anticipates utter genius in a biblical narrative I've written. While she will tell me what she doesn't like in my writing, she spends most of her time praising what she does. And with her by my side, what she imagines almost feels possible. She is by far my biggest fan.

Still, there are times when she gets anxious enough to see things in black and white. I have a fine-tuned Mom antennae and often receive her messages with sobering truckloads of salt.

"A brain surgeon? Isn't that just a little over the top?"

"All I know is when something wakes you up, it's really not good."

I didn't say anything. How does one rationally respond to that kind of homespun wisdom?

What I didn't take into account was that she was looking at me through the lens of the past several months: increasing naps, headaches, not feeling well. I could only hear her through the automatic assumptions of her typical overreaction.

January brought no relief. Instead, the pain and disorientation increased. Dr. Bentson's sinus infection theory was wearing thin—my symptoms were becoming more insistent. Finally, Greg and I listed everything we could think of that was bothering me, every symptom. And we made an appointment to see Dr. Bentson again for the afternoon of Friday, January 14th.

Friday morning, I drove to Portland's First Presbyterian Church to go to a workshop on worship. I found the church and drove around in search of a parking spot. Once out of my car, I had absolutely no idea where the church was. It was an intensely sunny day. I shielded my eyes from the sun where I stood on the sidewalk. I looked around in vain, searching for the church. The street became surreal and distant; my mind reeled in fear, trying to orient itself. Where was I? Where was the church? How could I lose such a huge building? Why was everything so far away? Why did everything seem so amazingly wrong?

My knees wobbled as I walked down the street. I had trouble keeping my balance, even as I held my head up and tried to look as if I was in control. As if nothing was wrong, as if I knew where I was going, as if it was simply a beautiful Friday morning. I tried to walk as if the sidewalk was not rocking out of control, as if my mind was not exploding with fear.

Just walk, Julie. This will all be OK. Just get to the church, they can help you there.

I finally found the church and stepped out of the bright sun into the dark entryway. There was a long, rectangular desk to the side, with a smiling woman behind it, asking me my name. I had to fight back the impulse to scream for help. I realized that, to her, I probably looked quite normal. I understood that this thing that was happening, this world that was coming apart, was only out of control for me.

When she looked up and handed me my nametag, I took it. I tried to pin it on my sweater, desperately wanting to look as normal as possible. *Hang on, Julie, the world will right itself in just a minute.*

Seeing friends and talking helped my brain to calm down and focus. I found my colleague and dear friend, Catherine, and we made plans for her and her husband to come our way for dinner that night. I told her of my mom's fears and my appointment later that day with Dr. Bentson, even as I made light of both.

"Dinner would be great. But if I have brain tumor, all bets are off—"

Catherine, ever rational, said in her teasing way, "Oh, it takes a few days to find out these things anyway."

Simply saying it out loud made it sound ridiculous. I felt foolish for even thinking it.

I was unwilling to consider what was clearly incredible.

Incredible.

I am struck by this word. "Credible" comes from the Latin *credere*, "to believe." If someone is credible, she or he is worthy of our faith, deserving of our trust. Reliable. In contrast, then, "incredible" is unbelievable, unreliable. One synonym for "incredible," according to my thesaurus, is "staggering belief." Shaking the foundational beliefs on which you've built your life. Up until this point, I trusted that I was God's child, and therefore God was looking out for me.

I believe some people are born to a certain life's profession. Greg is one of those people; I often joke that his DNA reads, (said in a high voice, while making a spiral movement downward with your index finger), "professor, professor."

When we met, he was a teaching assistant in the religion department at Pacific Lutheran University. While it was fun to play theological ping-pong, it was watching him teach a class that made me fall for him. He was an academic Robin Williams, firing off questions, making jokes, using film clips to demonstrate his point. This first morning I saw him teach, he was talking about what it means to be religious. If you define *religion* as the core value the drives an individual, everyone is religious. Everyone has something of ultimate value, that reason for getting up in the morning, whatever it is—money, status, a job—the thing in which they invest their lives. I watched him write on the chalkboard, checked out his butt, and thought, "I want him."

One of the classes Greg taught was on God and human suffering. The central question of the course was, "If God is good and powerful and loves us, how can there be such suffering in our world?" At the beginning of it, he asked his students to read Frederick Buechner's *A Sacred Journey,* Buechner's story of his journey with God. Then he had them write a brief, ungraded story of their own life with God. I don't know if it's because the assignment wasn't graded, or because students merely followed Buechner's lead, but Greg told me their stories were heartbreaking. Stories of incest, of the suicide of a sibling, of a mom's death to breast cancer. Life batters even the youngest among us, leaving them to conclude that God must not exist. "If there were a God, this never would've happened." Incredible. Staggering belief.

What I knew that strange December was that I did not feel well. What I did not know was that the cause of my distress was *incredible*. It would stagger my beliefs, beliefs that told me life was essentially hopeful and good, beliefs that promised bad things happened to other people, beliefs that seduced me into thinking I controlled my fate.

Friday afternoon, January 14th, Dr. Bentson listened to my list of symptoms. She gave me a neurological exam with pinpricks, and coordination tests used for suspected drunken drivers. "Stand up, close your eyes. Reach out your hand and touch your finger to your nose. Close your eyes and tell me if this is sharp or smooth. Walk across the room, one foot directly in front of the other . . ."

I was nervous that this test would show me something about myself that I didn't want to see. My competitive nature kicked in, and I tried my level best to be the pure embodiment of grace.

"Close your eyes. Reach out your hands in front of you, palms up." I peeked to make sure they were even. So far, so good. While she checked my reflexes with her little rubber hammer, she joked about how she should have become a neurologist—all the tools they need are a reflex hammer and a safety pin. Finally, she told me my exam was normal. But my relief was short lived; she ordered a CT scan of my head. I was instantly alarmed and pelted her with questions.

"If my exam is completely normal, why the CT scan?"

"Just a precaution to eliminate possibilities. Your exam was normal. I'm 99% sure the scans will be, too. Let's just do it so we can send copies to your family and calm everyone down."

In her notes for the examination on January 14, she wrote that my symptoms were mild, and attributed them to being "tired because she is a minister and worked hard in Dec. and doesn't have very much money and can't take a vacation." She did mention that "the double vision is a little bit worrisome. She had this before, and now it is coming back . . . it worries me and the new headaches have her and her family concerned too." She suggested the possibility there was something in the sphenoid sinus that could cause both problems.

Reading her notes years later, I was struck by two things. The first, how casual Dr. Bentson was. She really was not overly concerned, even though I was sleeping ten hours a night, and not feeling any better. But the second realization: she ordered the CT scan mostly to get a glimpse of my sinuses. Had I known this when she ordered my scan, my weekend would have been much more relaxed. But I only knew that I needed a CT scan of my brain, and that was reason enough to be afraid.

The relationship between reason and fear is a tempestuous one. Not everything reasonable is to be trusted. And not every fear is true. Sometimes reason can put fears to rest; other times fear will find solid ground for its torment. It has always been Greg's way to use reason to calm fears. "Why worry before we know anything?" he said several times that weekend. After all, my headaches could be anything: stress, sinuses, muscle spasms. I would later learn that double vision is a major indicator that something is seriously not right, but Dr. Bentson had assured me my exam was fine.

Part of me tried to believe she was right. *Yes, but what can anyone really tell with a safety pin and a walk across the floor?* And the prescription for my CT scan jumped into the debate—that square piece of paper declaring "headaches and double vision." Written like that it sounded so bad.

It was a fortune cookie that settled the debate. I was feeling so lousy that we had set up our ancient little black-and-white TV in the bedroom so I could stay in bed and watch. We had Chinese food Saturday night. I love fortune cookies, but when I opened mine, fear exploded in me. It wasn't the fortune itself—I have no idea what it said. It was the fact that when I looked at it, I could not read it. The lines danced over and around each other. I could only read it if I closed one eye. It might have declared "This is Your Lucky Day." But it would have been wrong.

I could no longer deny it. There was something seriously wrong in my head, there was something messing with my eyesight, and giving me headaches and making me dizzy. Trying to read that stupid little strip of white paper that called itself a fortune, I was terrified. Though I knew something was not right, I had no idea what that it meant to say that. Or what it would mean.

In Mark chapter 4, the disciples were tossed helplessly around in their fishing boat in one of the Sea of Galilee's notorious storms. The ancient people not only feared the water's thrashings; they also feared the sea demons that lurked just below the surface.

Jesus was sound asleep in the stern of the boat; in their fear, the disciples woke him.

"Help! Wake up! Don't you care that we're going to die?"

Awake now, Jesus offered them a fleeting glance. He turned his attention to the wind. In two words he rebuked their vengeance. Two simple words—Be Still—commands really, and the waters stilled. The boat settled.

The storm clouds had gathered in my life, the water was getting rough. All the reason in the world could not stop the winds of fear that grew stronger with each minute. I knew that something was beneath the surface. And it was serious. The demons were stirring up the waters of my life. Would the master of the sea be with me to command his word of rebuke? Would he be there to calm the storm?

2

⁗⁖⁖⁖⁖

Leaving the Garden

On Monday morning, January 17, Pam and I sat in my office and I told her of my Cat scan the following day. I was thinking of canceling the scan. It seemed an overreaction. Even as I was speaking, I knew she would not agree.

"Julie, you've had headaches for literally months."

"I know, but it could be anything, right? Sinus troubles can last for months, can't they?"

"I don't think so. And anyway, if there's nothing wrong, then you have nothing to worry about, right? I think you need to do this. If only so we can get closer to figuring out what's wrong. It doesn't take very long—just a few hours. Let's do this so we can move on."

If I had been honest in that moment, I didn't want to have the scan because I didn't want to know what the real problem was. In my case, not knowing felt a whole lot more safe than knowing—an irrational version of the whole "ignorance is bliss" thing. But the rational side of my brain knew that she was right. The sooner I had this test, the sooner I would be able to figure out what was going on and take steps toward getting better.

A few weeks before that, Pam's son Matthew had begun having unexplained headaches. His doctor finally suggested a Cat scan. The morning of his scan, I went to be with her at the imaging center, but we missed connections. Later, the news came back that the scans were clear. So on the morning of my scan, the waiting room with its comfortable couches initially felt warm and safe. It was as if Matt's going before me ensured that I too would have good news. And frankly, a part of me was embarrassed by all of the fuss.

The walls in the waiting room were a noncommittal yellow. An aged oil painting hung on the wall, a once a glorious ocean scene with waves crashing, the sun setting in the background. But the paint had started to fade, and the picture hung there reluctantly, almost apologetically. Crinkled magazines on the side table were old and well read. Pam, Greg, and I sat close together, trying to think of something to talk about. That in itself bothered me; Pam and I had never before run out of things to say. But here we sat. Small talk was impossible; we were here in this tired place, pondering the possibility of a scary thing. We were here waiting because I was going to have a test to find out if there was something wrong with my brain. I wasn't cold but I could not stop shivering.

Finally, a young man in a white coat came for me. He led me into a room with medical- supply boxes stacked up in the corners and on one of the counters. It smelled like plastic and Band-Aids and alcohol—the antiseptic variety. In the center stood this awkward contraption; it was a vertical ring about five feet in diameter with a thin table that stuck out of it horizontally, as if it were sick of being used and was sticking out its long, straight tongue in protest. The tech had me lie down on the skinny table, which was draped with a white sheet, and settled my head into a bracket. He centered a small infrared light from above the ring onto my forehead. Like a flight attendant giving the safety lecture for the zillionth time, he mumbled, "OK, so we're gonna take three scans and then we'll need to inject some dye for contrast, then we'll take three more. You just need to lay still, OK?"

He walked out, closed the heavy door, and stood behind a computer in the room next to me.

At least that is what I assume he did. I didn't actually see him. I was on my back, forced to contemplate the ceiling, my head imprisoned by the bracket. But the thought came to me, which comes every time the dentist steps behind a screen when taking an ex-ray, if it's not safe for him to be in the room with me, what in the world makes it safe for me to be in the room with me?

Zing! Zing! The ring spun around like a ride at the fair, zipping three hundred and sixty degrees one way, only to pause before it counterzipped the other way. I gritted my teeth and tried really hard not to think. But it seems when you tell your brain to shut up, as if it were a rebellious four-year-old, it only cranks the volume. *What am I doing here? How did I end up staring at this stupid ceiling? When will this be over so I can get back to my life?* The zinging stopped. The door opened, and I heard someone click-clicking her way toward me.

"Time for the contrast." She could not have been more cheery if she were giving me a spa treatment. "Let's find a good vein on ya." She laid my right arm on a tray, tightened a tourniquet around it, and started tapping the inside of my elbow.

"Oh man, that's a great twister! When you get old and are in the hospital, show them this twister, it's a really easy hit!"

She was so casual. Did that mean anything? Did people come in all the time to get scans of their heads?

I felt a prick, and then a tingling swooshed through my body. My face flushed and a metallic flavor invaded my mouth. She clicked her way to the door, slammed it, and the zinging began again. I took a deep breath, trying to relax. We were almost done. *Hang on, Julie, it's almost over.*

Finally, the young tech returned. What happened next taught me something: techs know more than they tell you. He wanted me to roll onto my stomach and place my chin in the plastic cup he put there to brace my head. They wanted more pictures.

"Why?" They hadn't told me about this.

"We think we see something. The radiologist wants to get a closer look." He sauntered out, closing the door behind him.

I shook and felt weightless, like a decayed leaf just waiting on the sidewalk for one strong blast of air or a stomp of a well-placed foot to finish it off. *This does not make sense. There is some kind of mix-up here. Some major mistake. There is nothing wrong in my head. Don't they get that? Nothing wrong!* Even as I mentally came to my body's defense, the small voice in the corner of my mind nodded. *Now everything makes sense.* I lay on my stomach, my chin balanced in the little plastic cup and felt instant, complete, horrifying fear. "We see something, but it looks like it's been there awhile."

I was alone. I was imprisoned in a room with no windows, separated from those strangers by dark glass and a closed door. Greg and Pam were an eternity away. I was completely alone in that otherworldly place.

My teeth chattered. My body quivered. There was something wrong in my head. *In my head.* What happens to you when there is something wrong inside your brain? If it was a breast or an arm, you could cut the thing out of it, or if worse came to worst, cut it off if you had to. But call me crazy, I'm thinking that's not an option when it comes to your brain. Brains are listed in the body inventory as Required Equipment

My mind became a whirling dervish, racing wildly, trying to make this "we think we see something" fit with the story that I clung to, that I was basically healthy, that there was nothing radically wrong with me. It was a story I was holding on to with less and less conviction, like when the Road Runner tries to save himself as he falls from a cliff by grabbing on to a rope, only to discover the rope's other end is not attached to anything. My thoughts landed on a woman I had met the previous year at the church. She told me she had a benign tumor in her brain that just needed to be operated on occasionally to keep its growth under control.

"Oh God, please let that be my story. Please let this be a benign, friendly tumor with no malicious intent to destroy my life. Please just let it be something that we can deal with and make go away."

Finally, the zinging stopped, the door opened, and the young tech told me I could get up, they were done.

I sat up, dizzy with fear. I could see a faint reflection of myself in the dark glass. I waited for the room to stop spinning, and then I gingerly stepped off the table and made my way to the room where the radiologist sat. He faced the computer; I looked over his shoulders. He pointed at a shadowy image that he assured me was my brain. The picture on the screen looked like a slice of an old growth tree trunk, with rings of muted grey. The radiologist pointed to a few white circles.

"See those? Those are way too big. Those are called ventricles, they're sacks holding your cerebral spinal fluid. They're way, way too big because they can't drain. It's as if you have water on the brain." Water on the brain, or Hydrocephalus, (literally Greek for "watery head") means that the flow of the Cerebral Spinal Fluid is somehow obstructed, blocking the ventricles from draining. The spinal fluid builds up in the brain's ventricles, or CSF sacks, and can cause headaches, nausea, vomiting, sometimes blurred vision and balance problems.

"They are not draining because of that," he said.

He directed my reluctant eyes to the white, oblongish thing in the middle of my brain. I stared at that damned spot. A shapeless blotch, like a broken egg, centered in my brain, at the core of command central. Suddenly, memories of the headaches, dizziness, double vision, confusion—they all flashed through my mind like a slideshow as if to say, "We were trying to tell you. Don't blame us. We tried, but you weren't listening."

The once cheery tech who'd delighted in finding my "twister" went and told Pam and Greg they could join me. When they came in they were both pale and wide-eyed with fear.

"I have something growing in my head."

I let out a quick sob as I walked into Greg's open, unbelieving arms.

"I want my life back."

I led them to the computer and the radiologist.

What the radiologist had explained was too hard to take in. The "impression" of Pathology Report reads:

"There is a large partially calcified mass arising in the posterior fossa in the region of the superior medullary velum which obstructs the fourth ventricle and causes hydrocephalus. This almost certainly represents a primary brain tumor. Several possibilities might be considered. Its proximity to the tentorial notch makes a meningioma a possibility. Arising near the fourth ventricle a dependymoma might also be considered. An intra-axial brain tumor would be most likely.

READ & APPROVED BY: ANTHONY G. PAPPAS, MD."

I stared at the screen and immediately recognized that my life was no longer in my hands—had it ever been? I stared at the screen and understood that my body—like life itself—was a mystery and essentially outside my control. We live our days mostly with the assumption that how we do it is up to us. And on the surface, this is true. And on the surface, we absolutely need to believe this—if not, how would any of us be able to get up in the morning? And even when we do admit to the vulnerabilities of fate—you never know, you could get up and get hit by a truck . . . you just never know—I think that's a nod to life's unpredictability, but only that. A glance. A quick awareness. The universe tapping us on the shoulder.

But I was staring at the inside of my brain. It was a two-dimensional view, flattened, like being squished between two slides under a microscope. And according to those who knew, it was not a normal sample. As I looked at the picture, as I listened to the radiologist talk about "water on the brain," deep in my heart, I knew it was true. My increasing confusion, my inability to read without closing one eye, all confirmed what I was looking at. And in that instant, my life was ripped apart from any quaint assumptions I held about my future. My assumptions that I would live into my eighties, that I could choose to have children, that I would be essentially healthy and happy, grow old with Greg, perhaps choose a different career—all burned away by the white thing lodged in the center of my brain. With that white spot on the screen, my world crumbled, like so much dust.

Greg and I married the December after I graduated (with an eminently marketable BA in English), and eight months later we packed our 1984 Honda hatchback Accord to the roof with all of our worldly goods and drove across the country to Princeton, New Jersey. In five days. I was a Seattleite to my bones, never having lived east of Washington State. Home to me meant rain and mountains and lakes and towering fir trees. Home to me meant great coffee and losing an umbrella on a weekly basis. Poor Greg! We hadn't been married a year and here was his new bride, sobbing her way through northern Idaho and eastern Montana. My eyes dried as I took in the vast, tennis-court flatness of the country. There were no speed limits in North Dakota. There were no hills, trees, rivers, mountains, bumps, curves, buildings, houses, gas stations, outhouses, or bushes. Not one thing that invited a person to stop and put her feet up, take a load off. Each "rest stop" was a spot of asphalt with a garbage can.

We finally pulled into one, and after hours and hours in the car, my legs protested at actually having to do something. The wind whipped through my poorly named windbreaker. I went in a futile search for a bathroom—maybe it was over there, behind that tumbleweed? Or perhaps there was a cleverly hidden hole in the ground? A woman stood by her car, her face worn by wind and dust and age.

"Where're ya' headed?" she asked, dragging on her cigarette.

"I'm leaving home. I'm going east to New Jersey." Fighting back the tears.

"Oh, honey. Home is where you hang your hat."

Princeton, New Jersey, is where my hat hung for three years. Princeton Seminary had a huge endowment, and when we got there my choices were (a) to work Greg through school, or (b) to go to school myself and let Princeton pay the bill. It didn't take a brain surgeon to figure that one out. With clear intentions, very, very clear intentions to not work in the church, I began the Master's of Divinity program, while Greg entered the PhD program in systematic theology.

When I came to Princeton, my initial thought was that I would use my theological education to write for some kind of Christian publication. To that end, I created my own internship with *The Other Side* magazine. *The Other Side* is a Christian magazine committed to looking at the world from the other side, from the point of view of the oppressed. It was not a magazine for the Religious Right, as it rarely mentioned being "born again"; the focus of *The Other Side* was the injustice of our culture. I remember one article the senior editor wrote titled "No More Prisons. Not One More." The magazine was radically committed to the poor.

The Other Side was housed in a walk-up in a terribly poor part of Philadelphia. Their door was always locked; so many days I shivered on the butt-cold sidewalk, ringing the bell, waiting for someone to come down the stairs to peek through the little slat in the door. Inside was not much better, as they did not turn the heat on, and we mastered the skill of typing with fingerless mittens. They paid their employees very little but provided first-class medical insurance.

My next year, when the seminary required me to work in a church, I wanted to work with a woman pastor in a small church. Laurie was in her thirties, was married to a doctoral candidate, had two young sons, and they lived across the street from the church in a big, old wooden house. She was a fantastic preacher, funny and relevant, and somehow not preachy. I still remember the sermon she preached on the seductive, secretive power money plays in our lives.

The church, in Palisades, New York, was a quaint country Presbyterian church that stood off the road a bit, surrounded by trees. If stuffed to the gills, it could probably hold all of eighty people. Its steep A-framed roofline, with a small cross at its peak, distinguished it from the few neighboring houses. It took me an hour and a half to get there each Sunday.

After my first Sunday service, I stood at the door, greeting people as they left, and through the blur of strange faces, a man walked by who looked vaguely familiar. At lunch with a member of the church, this woman said, "Did you just die when William Hurt shook your hand?" It turned out this little church was packed with actors, models, writers, and musicians who worked across the river in the city. One Sunday during the coffee hour, Gail, the woman in charge of the Sunday school program said, puffing out her cigarette smoke and gazing at Bill Hurt, "I don't care what anyone says, I still think he's got a flat butt."

Laurie was unlike any pastor I had known. First off, the fact that she was a woman with her own church was rare. And she was smart and irreverent in the best sense. Her sermons were simple, based on the Bible reading for the day, but utterly relevant. I loved Sunday mornings, and I began to think of the ministry as a viable life option.

Princeton required us to meet with the other interns and their mentor-pastors every month. Sitting in a room with balding, overweight, self-important men, my potential future colleagues, everything in me cried, "Run, Julie, Run!" But with Laurie assuring me these were not the people with whom I would work on a daily basis, and with the actual work of preaching and being with people coming so easily, I noticed that the relentless internal questioning that plagued me for months had quieted. The question shifted without my awareness from "What do I want to be when I grow up?" to "When I become a pastor I will . . . "

Graduating from Princeton Seminary in 1990, I took my first pastorate at the aging Presbyterian church in Albany, Oregon, as their associate pastor for children and young families. The church had not had a second pastor for a long time. The position of associate for families was a new position for them. Never mind that there was a dearth of young families with whom to minister. Never mind that there was one infant in the nursery cared for by a gentle, bent-over, aged woman who seemed perpetually confused about what, exactly, she was there for. Never mind that, looking out on the congregation, I saw waves of grey hair, bald heads, and blue hair.

The only thing that mattered was that this dwindling congregation was in Oregon. I was back where I belonged—with rain; good coffee; real mountains; and the wild, roaring Pacific Ocean within reach. So what if coming to this aging church was what it cost to be home? If there were no families, we'd just have to find them. I'd figure it out. Surely it wouldn't be that hard.

Someone paged Dr. Bentson. She came rushing across the street from the hospital in tears. I held her, wondering, what was wrong with this picture? How did it become my job to comfort her? Dr. Bentson, Pam, Greg, and I went into a small office. It was really just a file room. Tall grey filing cabinets stood in lines, their drawers all facing the same direction, standing at attention and ready for any important filing activity to commence. My back and Greg's back were up against the cabinets, Pam stood to the side. Dr. Bentson faced us, talking on and on. I remember little of what she said, but I do remember one thing. Dr. Bentson was talking in her characteristic fast, scattered way.

I waited for her to take a breath. "I'm not going to die," I said.

She looked away briefly and said, "Of course not." By that glance, I knew she wasn't sure. But I was.

It's important to know that in my family I am known for being stubborn beyond all reason. Maybe it's my mother's bulldog tenacity reborn in me. One November when I was in high school, I came home to announce I was going to sew my boyfriend a shirt for Christmas.

"But," my mom explained, "you don't know how to sew."

"I know, but it can't be that hard; women do it all the time."

I got the shirt done, though not without multiple ripped-out seams, angry screams, and several choice expletives. As I grew up, my general attitude was, if I put my mind to it, (and maybe, failing all else, read the directions), nothing was all that tough.

Standing among the gray file cabinets of the imaging center—wasn't there a better place for conversations like this?—I knew Dr. Bentson was not at all sure I would live. But to me, this was not open for debate. Even as I said the words, "I'm not going to die," I knew that an onlooker would say this was a classic response. According to Elisabeth Kübler-Ross, famous for her detailed descriptions of the stages of grief, denial is the first step. But that onlooker, be it Elisabeth Kübler-Ross or anyone else, didn't know me. No one knew the obstinacy that pulsed in my veins.

Refusing to die was one thing, but finding a way to stay alive was another. I did not know what this diagnosis meant for my life. Everything was instantly called into question. I knew that the daily rhythms of my life—work, home, friends—were stripped from me. I didn't know what would take their place. I no longer had the luxury of assuming that mostly good things would happen in my life. My life was no longer mine. Not mine to determine, to direct. And there would be many times over the next two years when nothing was mine to determine. But for that moment, just for an instant, I decided I would not die. What I intuited, though there was no way to know the details, was that this would be a fight. It would take all I had to face this.

Greg and I went home to call family. I broke the news to my parents. How do you "break" the news that you have a brain tumor?

"Mom, Dad—are you sitting down? I have some pretty bad news. I just had a Cat scan and discovered that I have a brain tumor . . ."

Mom gasped. Dad was silent.

"We know very little, so I can't really give you any details. But our plan is to take my scans to a few hospitals in Portland, and meet with some neurosurgeons to decide who will treat it."

"We're coming down right now," Dad said.

"Why don't you wait until we know more?" I suggested. There was no need for them to leave work until we knew the plan.

Right after we said goodbye the phone rang.

It was Dr. Bentson, sounding much relieved.

"I've talked with a few neurosurgeons in Portland. After describing the location of the tumor, both docs that I spoke to said most tumors in that region are benign.

"Pack a suitcase, you might be in Portland a while. And Julie? You're not allowed to drive. Make sure Greg drives, OK?"

On hearing this, I felt a deep sense of relief. *Finally, someone is going to help me.* Even though the news was unimaginably bad, I found some comfort in it. At least the monster had showed his face. I no longer had to deal with stormy waters and unknown demons.

I called my parents again. My dad picked up, and he was crying.

"Dad, why are you crying?"

Silence. "Because you have a brain tumor."

"Well, don't worry. I don't think it's that bad. Dr. Bentson just got off the phone with a few neurosurgeons in Portland. She described the location to them, and both said that most tumors in that area are benign. I don't think it'll be that bad."

The one-hour trip to Portland was a silent one. Neither Greg nor I could find much to say. Before that day, I had had only a vague awareness of Oregon Health Sciences University (OHSU). I knew it was a major research hospital and medical school, but that was pretty much the extent of it. What I did not know was that it was built on a hilltop with an unimpeded view of the city. The drive to it is a windy ascent, with mansions surrounded by beautifully manicured lawns. Most yards had roses, ancient majestic roses that would color the neighborhood in a few months. We drove past Washington Park, with its tennis courts and famous rose gardens. Why would such an important trauma center and teaching hospital be at the top of this crazy climb?

We wove our way through the maze of buildings that made up the OHSU campus to a newer building that smelled of wood, paint, new carpet—a smell I will always associate with that place.

In Dr. Johnny Delashaw's office, I was instantly perplexed that the waiting room was filled with people of all shapes and ages. *Why were so many people there?* I had no idea neurosurgeons had such thriving practices. Yet here they sat, calmly reading magazines in the waiting room of a *brain* surgeon. What could possibly be wrong with *their* brains? And even more confusing, why do they look so calm? I had seen more uptight people in the fast lane at the grocery store.

Whatever the problems of those patients, they must not have been as serious as mine. The minute the receptionist heard my name Greg and I were hustled into an examining room. Dr. Delashaw was young, good-looking, with dark hair and a baby face. He might pass for a doc on a television show, but a brain surgeon?

Dr. Delashaw put my Cat scans on the lighted wall, where they looked like Rorschach butterflies. He explained that he wasn't sure what he was looking at, and told us it was possible the tumor wasn't serious. He even said there was a good chance he could save my hair. An MRI would tell him more.

"MRIs are the coolest things," he said, as if I cared. "It's like looking at a two-dimensional picture with a Cat scan, and then having that picture explode into three dimensions. My job became a whole lot easier when MRIs came on the scene."

All I cared about was that he thought he could save my hair. *If he's talking about my hair, it can't be that bad, can it?*

He and I soon developed a joking banter.

"I gotta' tell ya', you look too young to be a pastor . . ."

"Well, I've gotta' tell you, you look too young to be a neuro-surgeon, and right now, I'm thinking that's a bit more important."

He called MRI.

"OK. Here's the deal. They were all booked up, but I told them you were really sick. You've gotta' act sick."

Wasn't I?

"How's this?" I grabbed my waist, bent over slightly. Grimaced.

"Work on it," he said.

Around corners, up a floor, across a walkway, we passed from one building to another in the maze of that amazing place. Down what looked like a service elevator in a hidden corner we came out into a small corridor. At the end, a sign: Magnetic Imaging Center.

"Look sick," he'd said to me. Didn't I? How could I not look sick when there was something foreign growing in the center of my head? But that's the particular maliciousness of this kind of attack. No outward signs witness to the growing intruder intent on consuming everything in its path.

The MRI machine was a vast, off-white plastic wall, with a long skinny table coming out of a narrow coffin-shaped hole. There was a soft beeping that coincided with the red blinking light at the top of the hole. Unlike the Cat scan machine, this machine was in a room entirely dedicated to its function. No storage boxes to be seen. No counters or cupboards. It faced a window behind which a computer reported what it saw. And because a Magnetic Imaging machine uses magnets to create an image, Greg could be in the room with me.

This time I shook for two reasons: I was scared, and I was really cold. I had traded my clothes for a flimsy hospital gown tied at the back. Providing warmth is not a part of the job descriptions for hospital gowns; providing privacy is about all they can do, and they don't do that very well. I found myself lying again on a small plastic table and wondering how in the world people who were fighting their weight could squish themselves onto it. When the tech saw me shaking, he brought over two gloriously warmed blankets and covered me from head to toe. The warmth calmed me; it was a kind gesture, a moment of grace. I breathed deeply.

Having a Cat scan is a day at the beach compared to having an MRI. Where the Cat scan is a wide ring in which your head rests, an MRI is a body-length, curved tube: a menacing, high-tech coffin. The top of the tube is only four or five inches above your nose. When they're scanning your head, a brace encircles it. There's a little mirror above your eyes that allows a glimpse down the tube and over your toes. This scan is not for the faint of heart, and those who suffer from claustrophobia are often sedated. Depending on which body part is to be scanned, an MRI lasts between an hour and an hour and a half.

After I was slipped into the tube, only my feet were free of it. Greg rubbed them and held them as the test started. It started slowly with a few knocks, but quickly kicked up to a fast jack-hammer-like pounding. There was a screaming high-pitched metallic sound just beside my head, as if the test was to see how long one could stand the pounding.

I tried to distract myself.

Pray, Julie. Pray. How? How can one focus on anything, trapped in this terrifying, solitary place? What is this torture chamber, some kind of prelude to a coffin? Stop thinking that! God, Julie! Stop it. Pray. Use the alphabet. O.K., all right. . . . I pray for Andersons, for answers, for being better. How'd you like that? A little alliteration, huh? I pray for the church, the congregation—when will this pounding stop?—for Carla, Cory, . . . what do they see? . . . When will I get out? For Dad, deliverance—I can't do this. Yes you can! You're doing it. Keep it up! We will be out of here sooner or later. Pray!! I pray that this is curable—oops, sorry that was a "c". That it's all going to be OK., something insignificant. I pray that I would wake up and this would all be a bad dream. A vivid dream, but a dream all the same.

During the pounding, I strained to hear some assurance. But there was only silence in the midst of the pounding. I looked at the little mirror that reflected the images at my feet. Beyond the tops of my toes, I saw the shadows of people moving around in the adjoining room. I knew the images of my brain were on their screen. It seemed so ultimately wrong that they knew what I did not. What news? What news?

How long is an eternity? Why does it seem that time stops when a stranger knows more about your destiny than you do? Eternity is the suspension of time. The focus of attention, soul, on the silence of no-word.

Once out of the horror machine, I sat up, and through the shadows, saw Dr. Delashaw in the MRI office. He was looking at the pictures of my brain. Shoulders slumped, head down. Bantering energy gone. I knew it was not good.

When Greg and I met him outside the computer room, I asked, "It's not good, is it?"

No response. I asked him, "What do you see?"

Silence.

And in that silence, he spoke more than I wanted to hear.

Back in his office, he lit up the scans on his light wall. How can this be my brain? It looked more like a kid's art project, where you paint one side of a piece of paper and then fold it, making a really weird goopy butterfly.

"There, see how the white mass is squiggly here? I'm not sure it's a benign tumor. It could be benign. Or it could be something else. I'm not sure what it is. It may take two surgeries to get it all."

Answers that are no-answers are the most terrifying of all.

When Greg and I came out of Dr. Delashaw's exam room, Mom and Dad were there in the waiting room. How did they get here so fast? Mom and Dad were *here*. Not in Seattle, at work, where they belonged. But here in this Portland hospital, in the waiting room of Dr. Johnny Delashaw, brain surgeon. Another wave washed over me. *This is really happening. This is real.*

Johnny showed them my butterfly brain. He tried to explain what he didn't know, and said he would admit me the next day. The morning after that, surgery. Brain surgery.

Journal, May 1994

As I was sitting in church Sunday, it struck me: Greg and I have been kicked out of the garden. We were together, boldly trying to live our dreams, assuming the world— (for us, at least—I am ashamed of our egocentrism)— the world was a safe and good place.

But with my tumor, we have etched upon our hearts the fundamental fragility of life. (And so I jump at wayward cars and am a bit more fearful at just about everything.) The garden of our security, the garden of our hopes, grounded in the assumption that life will be good for us—(God will be good to us?)—is closed to us forever. We are outside the gate, in a mysterious and unfamiliar world, where, as Bill Cosby says, "at 10 o'clock the monsters come out . . ."

Greg and I had stepped out into a world we did not know. How, then, do we live? We reached for each other's hands, and I thought of Adam and Eve leaving the garden, so masterfully portrayed by Milton in *Paradise Lost*.

The world was all before them, where to choose
Their place of rest, and providence their guide;
They hand in hand, with wand'ring steps and slow,
Through Eden took their solitary way.[1]

1. John Milton, *Paradise Lost*, 12.646–49.

3

⁊ᒪᒧ

Hope & Prosperity

The next day, Wednesday, January 19, was a bizarre day. Or, better put, it was just one more bizarre step in a nightmare that seemingly had no end. The day was a bitter, teeth-chattering cold. The sky was a deep crystalline blue. I sat in the reception area of the hospital, waiting to be admitted, and watched people pass me as they walked through the main hospital doors. Medical students with their ever present clipboards and swift pace. Older patients in their hospital gowns, let out to have a cigarette. A small group of nurses, just outside the doors, smoking. Doctors conferring with each other, carrying paper coffee cups. People entering for the first time—you could tell because they stopped—looked all around, before heading to the receptionists.

As the people walked by, I couldn't help but wonder about their brains. That woman there, in the pink scrubs and with a definite purpose to her steps—did she have a normal, functioning brain? *Yes. Of course her brain is working within normal parameters—she's walking a straight line, talking with the person next to her. They both laugh. How* could *there be anything wrong in her brain?* Well, I shot back, I can do all of those things right now, I can walk, run, dance. I can tell a joke, have some lunch. And yet, I don't have a normal, functioning brain. And it is so critical that I may never again have a carefree day, where my biggest dilemma would be what to fix for dinner. I may never again have the luxury of simply going to work. On the outside, I looked just like them. But in that moment, I could not have been more different. There I sat because my life hung in the balance. I sat waiting to be admitted, so that tomorrow I would have brain surgery.

I sat there because if I didn't, I would surely die.

At the admission desks of most hospitals a small sign sits off to the side, "Please inform the receptionist if this is a work-related injury." Every time I saw that little sign, I had to hold myself back from screaming, "YES! This is a work related injury! Let me tell you about it!"

Almost a year before my diagnosis, Chuck, the senior pastor at the church, left for a new position in San Diego. Typically, when the senior pastor of a Presbyterian church leaves, the congregation is required by the Presbytery to hire an interim pastor—someone to take over the position for about a year, and to help the congregation set loose its ties to the former pastor. To keep things from getting messy, the interim pastor cannot be considered for the permanent position. To save the money they had budgeted for Chuck's salary, the church created a position for me, "bridge interim pastor," which essentially meant that I would function as the interim Head of Staff for several months. Because I had been with them for several years, the learning curve was short. There was energy and life in the worship services; attendance remained strong.

In the fall, a few congregants decided that it would be only proper if the church hired an interim senior pastor. A few members of the church formed a small committee and, knowing of a man who was unemployed and an experienced interim, hired him.

There was a reason no church had hired him to be a permanent pastor. When he came, he changed everything in the congregation, from the worship bulletins to how Pam conducted the front office. His office was down the hall a bit from Pam; he could hear her conversations with congregants on the phone, and when she was finished, would tell her what she should have said. During staff meetings he would stare at our breasts; I had to request that he make eye contact with me on more than one occasion. He told dirty jokes during Sunday morning services, and during the year he was there, attendance at Sunday services plummeted from 350 to around 70.

I was enraged. I complained to the Presbytery office and was told by one executive that this new interim, A.C., was a "fuck-up." I watched the life of the congregation wither, like a plant that finally gives up without being watered. At my own peril, I protested in any way I could. I was in crisis; I was drowning. I watched him dismantle all of the ways we'd been the church—from changing how we worshiped to our church newsletter to how we functioned as a staff. I fought him at every turn, not thinking about potential payback.

Hospital reception was on the ninth floor, as was the neurology wing. On the neurology wing, the fading linoleum floors and the pale weather-beaten walls spoke of a long history of use. Files balanced precariously on top of one another in the nurses' station. The whiteboard with patient and doctor names listed was cluttered with notes about times and medication.

The walk to my room took a few nervous steps. Down the hall and to the left. Third room on the left. While Greg and I walked, I was again surprised at how busy the neurosurgery wing of the hospital was. We had to weave our way between the nurses and docs who moved swiftly among themselves, in a kind of awkward dance; each had somewhere to be and someone to see. Interns made notes on their clipboards, nurses' aides pushed carts in and out of rooms.

I spotted people in their beds, in various stages of horizontalness. Some heads were bound in bandages, some bald. Others not telling, covering their heads with glorious silk scarves. In contrast, I felt out of place. I looked the part of an apparently healthy woman, no bandages, no tippy gate, no walker to help me make it down the hall. I glanced into these rooms and knew that in the very near future I would be one of them, lying in my own bed with a bandaged head, watching people walk past my room.

News travels fast, and bad news travels like lightning. That afternoon, people came from all over the Portland area to see me. My hospital room was so small, most had to wait their turn in the hall. There were two beds in this room; mine was by the window, so I could look out on the city. How nice, I thought. A room with a view. It could reasonably hold two or three visitors squished around the bed. The receptionist at the front desk told me later, people would walk up, begin, "I'm here to see Julie L . . ." and before they finished speaking, she would point them down the hall.

Sitting in that bed, all I could think was how absurd this all was. Wasn't it five days before that I thought I might cancel my Cat scan? Wasn't it only a few days ago when I was one of the normal ones, talking with Catherine, wondering about what we would have for dinner? Yet here I was, feeling like a new exhibit at the zoo. "This just in: from the remote southern part of Africa, come quick, come while you still have time, check out Julie with a brain tumor, this may be your last chance." It felt like a huge mistake. I didn't feel that bad; really I didn't. But everyone was making such a big deal about it. People kept coming, standing around in little groups as if at some bizarre cocktail party. That in itself was so weird. A party in the neurological wing of OHSU? The only things missing were the requisite glasses of wine and delightful cheese puffs. My friends were crowding in, talking and laughing. They squeezed their way to me to give me a hug. In my hospital gown, I felt underdressed for the occasion.

When there was a lull, Dad broke out a deck of cards, Steve got some M&Ms to use as chips, and we played poker on my bed.

My brother Steve was two years older than me, and I had always considered him a childhood tour guide. I watched him go to grade school, survive middle school, find lifelong friends in high school. It was as if he broke trail for me. He was my hero from the beginning.

When my young parents became pregnant with him, they knew his name before he was born.

"Stevie kicked this morning," my mother would tell my dad.

Or "Stevie is sure getting big!" my dad would exclaim.

In one photo album, there is picture of my mom, all of twenty years old and six months pregnant, beaming as she stands on the foundation of what would be their new house. Mom's handwriting declares, "Stevie and the house under construction!"

His name would be Stephen, and he would be their perfect little baby. And it seems that even before he was born, he had a knack for meeting their every expectation. He was a boy, and he was perfect. He cried only when he absolutely had to. He slept through the night at a few months. His curious eyes took in everything; he laughed easily. He was delightful, so delightful, that thinking this parenting gig was a piece of cake, two years later they decided to have another.

That would be me.

This time there was no clarity as to which gender I was. This was back in the day when a pregnancy test was positive when the rabbit died. Further, they had no name for me while I was in utero.

Dad tells the story of pacing in the hospital waiting room while mom was giving birth to me. The room was mostly empty, worn-out chairs sat along the walls and a small table in the corner held a tired pile of old news magazines. There was another man waiting, a "hippie" my dad described, who, after watching Dad circle the room, at one point said, "You know what day it is, don't you?" My dad stopped, considered the man in the tie-dye shirt and long, messy hair. He shook his head. "It's Friday the thirteenth. Kinda' makes you wonder what they'll turn out like, doesn't it?"

While my brother was blessed with a name and the adoration due his perfection, I was crowned with a mischievous old wives' tale.

And a name they came up with on the spot.

"I didn't really like the name Julie that much, but we had to come up with something to get you out of the hospital" my mom explained to me one time. "But as I've gotten to know you, I like it a lot better."

"Julie." It was Johanna, a good friend from the church, on the phone. "How are you?"

"You know, I'm great except for the little problem of this brain tumor." And the weird thing was, that was the truth. I didn't feel bad, certainly not bad enough to warrant all the fuss. And I confess I am a party animal to the bottom of my toes—I loved having all my friends around. How fun was that?

My friends came to see me, and I have no doubt they came because they cared about me. For all any of us knew, this might be their last chance to be with me. But I also think there is something incredibly frightening and fascinating when a crisis of extraordinary proportions happens. Like with a multiple-car crash on the highway, we slow down to get a good view. To see what happened, to see if there are any survivors, to give thanks that it wasn't us in the flattened Accord. When life deals a blow so unexpected, so unwarranted, and so terribly threatening, we are scarily reminded of how little control of our lives we really have.

And there, on January 19, 1994, "normal life" was suddenly interrupted by stunning news. It was so awful, my friends had to know more. How could anyone resist? And this news was faith staggering; I was young, energetic, only twenty-nine years old, and I had a brain tumor. Clearly, if it could happen to me, it could happen to anyone. In that moment of crisis, my body, my life became an object lesson. If it could happen to me—someone who didn't eat red meat or pork, who exercised religiously, who drank very little—it could happen to anyone.

It is human nature to be stunned by life's incredible moments.

As they held my hand, or gave the top of my head a quick kiss, I knew the fundamental difference between myself and my friends: they were going home to their beds; they were going to wake up in the morning, have some coffee, go to work. My morning would be different, to say the least. I was going to be sedated, and Johnny (we started calling him Johnny after the hours he'd spent with us), Johnny, was going to cut into my brain.

Johnny was going to cut into my brain.

I wondered what forces in the universe had conspired to put me in that bed. Did I unintentionally piss off some god—the god of brain tumors, perhaps? Was I just a little too cavalier about my life? In my less sarcastic moments, in my lucid, rational moments, I realized I had done nothing to deserve this. At the same time, there was no way I could excuse myself from this. What gave me the right to exclude myself from something that happened daily to others?

Still, I think a central egocentrism operates in all of us, a perspective that says terrible things, illness, tragedy—they happen to someone else, not me. Perhaps psychologists would bless this self-centered perspective as normal, part of the survival gear we're born with.

But there are implications to this "not me" thinking. One is our compulsive need to explain illness. She had a heart attack because she was overweight and had high blood pressure. Why did he get cancer? Because he smoked too much, or maybe he had bad genes. She got sick because she was too stressed out. He got ill because he never dealt with his traumatic childhood. He got cancer because he never quite got his act together.

Of course with many illnesses there is a direct link between cause and effect. No doubt, discovering the cause of illness is one step towards eradicating it. Further, we make lifestyle choices all of the time that have a direct affect on our health for good and ill.

But it is also true that many illnesses have yet to be linked to specific, controllable causes. When we link their onset to a character trait, we step onto shaky ground. Dr. Bernie Siegel is a doctor whose life work has been with cancer patients. In the 1990s, when he was deep into his work, he kept his head shaved as a way to relate to his patients. He wrote a well-read book, *Love, Medicine and Miracles*, about living with and perhaps even beating cancer. Before I was diagnosed, I had visited a woman in our church who had cancer. When I saw Siegel's book on her coffee table, I felt a bit of hope for her. I was happy she was reading something constructive about her illness.

But then, when I was diagnosed, I read *Love, Medicine and Miracles*. And I became very, very angry. In it Siegel had the audacity to describe the psychological profile of someone who gets cancer.

> The typical cancer patient, let's say a man, experienced a lack of closeness to his parents during childhood, a lack of the kind of unconditional love that could have assured him of his intrinsic value . . . As he grew up, he became strongly extroverted, but not so much from an innate attraction to others as from a dependency on them for validation of his own worth. Adolescence was an even harder time for this future cancer patient than for other teenagers. Difficulty in forming more than superficial friendships led to an excruciating loneliness and reinforcement of earlier feelings of inadequacy.
>
> Such a person tends to view himself as stupid, clumsy, weak, and inept at social games or sports, despite real achievements that are often the envy of his classmates . . .
>
> At some time, however, usually in the late teens or early twenties, the patient-to-be falls in love, finds one

or two close friends, gets a job that provides real satis-
faction, or otherwise reaches some level of happiness
based outside the self. He is unable to take any credit for
this turn of events . . . As an adult, he is still character-
ized by a poor self-image and passivity regarding his
own needs . . .[1]

Siegel describes a lifelong pattern of denying the self for the
sake of another. He calls cancer the "disease of nice people." Let's
blame cancer on a person's lack of self-esteem, lack of feeling loved,
need to please people. To be fair, Siegel's point is that our illnesses
can teach us something about our lives. I don't disagree. But the
presumption behind his message is unacceptable: if you lived your
life differently, or, if you took the time to get your life figured out,
you might not have gotten sick. It is your fault.

Here is a man who somehow thought he had the right to judge
my life. But he knew jack about me. His audacity was misplaced,
offensive, and destructive. What made me most angry, though,
was his violation of the people he was trying to help. Here was a
man who had gained the trust of vulnerable, sick people. Here was
a man who had never had cancer himself, yet who explained away
the cause of this out-of-control, threatening monster by blaming
the victim. Wagging his cancer-free finger in our faces—*tsk, tsk.*

Blame is the last thing a cancer victim needs. There is already so much about the disease that sets one apart from "normal,
healthy" people. A bald head, the nausea, the compromised immune system from the chemo drugs. The treatments make one's
life a rollercoaster of feeling pretty much OK and then having to
get hit again with the poisons that ravage your body, poisons that
are designed to kill your cancer but make you feel the treatment
is worse than the illness. To suggest, by inference, that the victim
brought this suffering on herself is beyond insensitive.

1. Bernie S. Siegel, *Love, Medicine & Miracles: Lessons Learned about Self-
Healing from a Surgeon's Experience with Exceptional Patients* (New York: Harper
& Row, 1986) 92–93.

All in an attempt to set oneself apart from the cancer patient. If we can explain it, we can control it. If we can control it, we can contain it. Then we can make sure it won't happen to us. All of this is to quiet the fear that nibbles on the edge of our consciousness, whispering, "It *could* happen to you . . ." No, it feels much better to assign blame, be it secondhand smoke, diet, or personality. Then we can safely separate ourselves from illness and from those who are ill. We can define the sick as somehow *other*, and live with the false comfort that we are immune. But that's after you have a peek, to see just how bad it is, to see how the forces of nature can mess with your life.

That January afternoon, at the moment of crisis, people crowded the hospital to have a peek.

It was so hard for me to get that I was the multicar accident on the freeway. As people came and went, there were moments when I was overwhelmed by the shock and fear of it, and then there were other moments when I reveled in having a good poker hand or laughing at someone's joke.

When a traumatic experience happens to a child, the child talks about it over and over again, each time as if for the first time. There was a little girl in our congregation whose father died unexpectedly when she was three years old. "My daddy died yesterday," she would tell me each time she saw me.

"Yes, honey. I know, I'm so sorry."

Then the next time I saw her, "My daddy died yesterday."

"Yes, honey. I know and I'm so sad for you. Can I give you a hug?"

It was as if it took waves and waves of saying it for her little heart to really understand what it meant. Maybe because the concept of death is not something we're born with. It could be that the whole idea of death was too big for a little one who had just started living.

In a similar way, it took waves and waves of awareness to understand what was happening to me. Perhaps the concept of death is too big for any human heart to really get. Maybe because the human heart's sole job is focused on the business of living.

As I sat on the bed in a flimsy hospital gown with my friends surrounding me, there were moments when I simply could not believe what was happening. My mind could not get around the concept that there was something growing in it. I had to keep reminding myself that if I wanted to live, I had to stay in that bed. And close my eyes and grit my teeth and face the morning.

Because I am an ordained Presbyterian pastor, there was the obligatory visit from the office that governed the regional group of churches: the Presbytery. The woman who came to visit me was the Presbytery Executive. I knew her, but not well. By the time she arrived, most of my visitors had left, the lights had been dimmed, and the floor was quieting down. Only my family was present.

Her coming was ill timed. The moment for casual visits had passed. My party hostess inclinations were long gone, as the minutes marched relentlessly towards the morning and my craniotomy. I had no emotional energy to be gracious. And yet, pastoral rules being what they are ("the pastor, acting as a representative of both the congregation and God, is expected to visit, especially in crisis events"), we went through the motions. For whose benefit I did not know.

Her visit with me could've come right out of a pastoral care textbook. It might read:

> Chapter Three:
> Making those scary hospital visits:
>
> Come into the hospital slowly to give yourself time to assess the situation. Are family members present? How do they look? Is there a doctor in the room? When appropriate, sit beside the patient. Ask how the patient is feeling and express your deep shock and sorrow at the situation. Then read from your Psalter, (Psalm 23 is always a good one.) assure her of God's care. Offer a prayer. And because lingering can be terribly awkward,

explain that you have another appointment, but that you
will hold the patient in your prayers.

She held my hand, said a brief, heartfelt prayer, and was gone.

That night, the night before my brain surgery, the neurology floor was quiet. Nurses and the occasional doctor spoke with softer voices. The phones rang less. Just Greg. Just my family: Mom, Dad and Steve, and my sister-in-law, Jody. Then Pastor Ron came. Seeing him plod down the hallway with his bowlegged gait lifted my heart.

I give Ron most of the credit for my marriage.

The fall of my senior year, I moved back into the dorm early, as I was a resident assistant. Two years before, during my sophomore year, things had become serious between Greg and me, and he finally had to take seriously his list of the perfect mate.

It was a list he'd made before he started college, imagining the ideal life partner. He showed it to me when we first started dating, and we laughed, because I broke every single requirement.

1. Don't date someone older or younger than you.
2. Date someone who shares the same beliefs.
3. Date someone who has had the same life experiences as you.
4. No long-distance relationships.

While I loved Greg for his idealistic belief that he thought he could control his life to such an extent, another part of me naturally assumed he wasn't serious.

I was a junior at Pacific Lutheran University when Greg began his Master's of Divinity at Princeton, and he had a decision to make: throw out his way of seeing the world and commit himself to a life he didn't know, or stay with his view of the ideal relationship and let me go. Downsize me. Set me free to seek other options.

The list won.

My heart broke.

Fall of my senior year I'd heard through mutual friends that Greg was in Portland, Oregon, and half wondered if he would come by before he went back to Princeton. Even though he'd written me almost every day during the previous summer, his letters were about his work in the south. I had no idea what he was thinking about us.

He finally showed up one day, and we went to the zoo. As we walked by the elephants, he held my hand. When we came to the big cats, he let it go. Rounding the corner to the monkeys, he'd grab it again.

Back on campus, I said, "It was great to see you. But I'm done with this."

Shocked, he took a step back.

"What do you mean?"

"I'm through with the whole on again, off again, thing. I love you, but you know what? It's time for me to move on. I'm just not going to wait around any more."

He got a panicked look on his face and said, "I'll be back." He took off.

In twenty minutes, he was back.

"Come on, Julie. We need to go talk with Ron."

I debated with myself. I was curious what they had talked about. By this time, Ron was no longer chaplain at the school, but he lived a few blocks from campus and had a little funky office set up in his garage. It was in an old wooden garage, the kind of place that had soaked in the northwest rain for so long, it was perpetually damp. But Ron had carved out a small space, set up a desk, and had a little wood-burning stove. There was a weathered Chinese rug on the cement floor. Stuffed bookshelves provided shelter on one side. He had pictures of his two kids on the desk. Books teetered in two piles on either side of his desk.

"So." He looked at us and chuckled. "Have you two ever talked about what you want in a marriage?"

For a second I was speechless.

I shivered and moved closer to the stove.

"What on earth are you talking about? I just told this man to get out of my life, and you're talking about marriage? You're nuts!"

Nodding, he said, "I'm sure there're a lot of people who would agree with you. But I was just wondering. Maybe you'll find out that you really have different ideas about it all, but maybe you won't. I was just thinking it might be something you'd want to talk about."

Greg went back to Princeton, and we spent the fall talking. Not about marriage, never about marriage, but mostly about the details of our days. Sunday mornings after church, I wrote him letters. He would call weekly. Meanwhile, I dated other men. I spent a few evenings with an old boyfriend. I'd hang out in the dorm rooms of other friends. We'd go out for Mexican food. I had one friend I went running with. He was clean cut and would've fit in nicely with the *Happy Days* cast; he was sweet but clueless. He seriously freaked me out one day when he mentioned how his mom would approve of me for a daughter-in-law because of my low-sugar diet.

Still, it was fun to check out the world of men.

And then Greg would call.

In January that year (against the protests of my parents: "They have bars on the windows!! It's way too dangerous!") I took a class at Union Seminary in New York City: "Doing Theology at the Crossroads." I loved the city. I loved the energy, the constant motion, the wild traffic, and the incredible mixture of people that pounded the pavement. We stayed in the seminary dorms, visited different ministries for the down and out, and heard speakers tell of the many needs of the poor. On weekends I took the one-hour train ride to Princeton to visit Greg. It was a beautiful, sprawling campus with its trademark black squirrels jumping along the grass. I called it "Doing Theology at the Country Club."

In the last week of January my class finished. Greg and I drove up into the snowy hills of New England, mostly staying at sweet little B&Bs. Each day we would pick our next town to visit. Our guidebook was a hit-and-miss kind of thing, and I remember going to one recommended bed and breakfast and pulling up to this little yellow shack with a small sign dangling from a hook.

"Wow!" Greg said. "Welcome to the cot and cracker!"

I can't be sure, but I seriously doubt the M-word ever came up that week, though I do remember talking about who would balance the checkbook.

We married the December after I graduated.

I don't know how Ron got the word, but he drove the three hours from Tacoma to be with us in the hospital. Ron, Greg, and I went to a lounge to be alone. We sat in a circle, holding hands. I had a sense that there were many ways to go on this journey, some better than others. I understood that how I traveled through it would have an impact on who I would be at its end. Greg and I promised, in front of Ron, to help each other on the way. Ron gathered us up in his prayer.

Then he said, "As I drove down tonight, I thought about your lives. Two words came to me, two words that speak to how your lives have gone. One: *hope*. The other: *prosperity*. Not prosperity in the financial sense. But prosperity in the true sense: *pro spiritus*. Moving towards the spirit. I have always seen your lives as moving towards the spirit."

That first night in the hospital, as my parents were leaving, I asked Mom if she could make a poster while I was in surgery with the words *hope* and *prosperity* on it.

Finally, everyone left.

I was alone, left to sleep if I could.

On January 19, 1994, Dr. Johnny Delashaw wrote in my chart:

> Patient seen and examined. Large Pineal region tumor and hydrocephelas. Plan prescription full vent (?) suboccipital tumor with biopsy or resection of tumor depending on path. Risks [coma, stroke, death] and benefits discussed and patient agrees to proceed.

The next morning, Greg sat with me in pre-op, a large room divided into little rectangular spaces by flimsy curtains. The ceiling was at least eighteen feet high. It was bright and cheery in a way; a lot of natural light came through the broad windows along one wall. Before I went into surgery, I wanted to talk to Johnny. I wanted him to know he should take it all out. I was hoping against hope that this surgery would be the end of the story. I jumped off the gurney, which in itself took a measure of grace—how to do it, while simultaneously keeping my pathetic little hospital gown closed in key places and dragging my IV pole with me. I called his office. He was unavailable as he was prepping for surgery. I left a message with one of the nurses. Tell him to go for it; take it all out if he can.

I climbed back on the gurney. My empty stomach protested its missing breakfast with a defiant rumble. Greg sat next to me while we waited. I looked into his eyes and wondered, what do you say to the one you've loved for eight years? What do you say when this might be the last time you will be together? I feared death mostly because that would mean I would leave him, and I did not want to leave him. I was not ready to say goodbye. Greg told me later that the day of my surgery was the most important day of his life. More important, even, than the day of our wedding, because after eight years, he knew what it would mean to lose me.

Then, as Greg held my hand, a nurse put something in my IV. I fell asleep.

4

Hymns to the Silence

In the beginning was the Word, and the Word was with God,
and the Word was God.
He was in the beginning with God; all things were made through him, and
without him was not anything made that was made.

—John 1:1–2

ONE CENTRAL way the Bible imagines creation is that God brings order out of chaos. And that order comes through the spoken word. God created with a word. God said "Let there be . . . " and there was. It is the ultimate power, the word. It brings definition, it provides specificity: not this but that.

The room was bright, with orange-brown walls. I could barely open my eyes, squinting to keep the light out. I peeked around. With my extremely limited observational skills, I tried to scope out where I was. The first observation, that I was conscious and able to observe was great news. I'd survived my first, and hopefully last, cranioto-my. *Good for you, Julie!* I patted myself on my metaphysical back. *You're still alive! Way to go!* A machine beeped out an insistent rhythm to confirm my observation. My IV pole stood by like a faithful dog, my ever-present companion. There was something at-tached to my head; I moved my head just a little bit; I did not know if moving it would rip out some vital, life-sustaining tube. My legs were being squeezed alternately up and down by some torture contraption. I was at a slight incline. There were no windows in this place. Without natural light to ground me, I had no idea what time it was or even what day it was. I felt no pain. A nurse came in to fiddle with something attached to the top of my skull. It was a gentle tug, like when I was little and my mom was trying to get a knot out of my hair.

Then there was a man standing next to my bed, bending over and talking to me. A vaguely familiar face. Loud and energetic, trying to get my attention. A woman behind him held something out to me. I discovered later it was a basket of chocolate-covered pretzels. I had gone to seminary with the man and barely knew either of them. Yet there they were, asking me how I felt.

A stranger and chocolate pretzels? That's how I woke from this nightmare? While I was happy to be conscious—that could only be a good thing after a craniotomy—I was devastated that the first faces I saw were those of near strangers. To get them away, I turned and groaned. That was enough for the nurse to know some-thing wasn't right.

"Are you family members?" she demanded.

I heard indistinct mumbling.

"Get out of here. Now. Only family members are allowed."

"We'll leave these for you," the woman said, gesturing to the basket. "I hope you like them."

The thought that chocolate-covered pretzels could be any help in the intensive care unit after brain surgery was too absurd to acknowledge. I was intent on more crucial matters. I wanted to know what had happened. I remembered that the last words I sent to Johnny, before I was rolled into surgery, were to tell him to go for it. To get as much of the tumor as he could. Get it out of my head. Thinking back on that now, it is kind of funny, isn't it? Me telling a neurosurgeon how to do his job. But that morning, it was terribly important to me that he know where I stood. I clung fiercely to the hope that this tumor could simply be cut away.

But it was not to be.

I am told that those who came to wait out the day with Greg were hoping for a 12–15 hour vigil. If the surgery lasted several hours it meant that Johnny was working on cutting out the tumor. The longer the wait, the more hope they would have.

Years later, Steve told me that the phone in the waiting room rang after about two hours. Greg picked it up, found out they were backing out of my head.

"Shit" he said.

Mom wrote to me later of that day:

> [During surgery] when we got the news that the tumor was malignant, (I don't remember who told us . . . seems like it came from the operating room to the phone in the waiting room) they said they were backing out and were not trying to get any more of the tumor because it could do more harm than good—that they'd never really be able to get all the cancer cells that way anyway. I ran out of the waiting room, outside and down a sidewalk because I just had to get far away from that news . . . just run away from it because it was just too devastating to have to face.

The tumor was the size of a walnut. Johnny cut out about a third, but realizing that it was malignant and had wrapped around my brain stem, there was no point in risking further damage. It literally had a death grip on my brain. This tumor was declaring the terms of this battle. And it meant to win.

Worse still, Johnny did not know what kind of tumor it was.

More answers that were no answers. His were empty words that brought no light to my darkening world.

I had no way to think about this. A proverbial deer caught in the philosophical headlights, I was stunned to silence.

I could not pray.

Like a prompter standing on the side of the stage whispering a line to a stuck actor, hymns can help us to pray the words our hearts have forgotten. It is often said, the one who sings prays twice. And because hymns gave me the words I did not have, I closed my eyes and sang hymns to myself.

> Love divine, all loves excelling,
> Joy of heaven to earth come down,
> Fix in us Thy humble dwelling,
> All Thy faithful mercies crown!
> Jesus, Thou art all compassion,
> Pure, unbounded love Thou art;
> Visit us with Thy salvation,
> Enter every trembling heart[1]

The days after the surgery were a confused mix of trying to get my body back to some semblance of normal, sitting up more, getting out of bed just long enough to use the bed pan, forcing down disgusting hospital food, all the while trying to get my head around the fact that not only could this tumor not be cut away, it was ferociously set on destroying me by invading my mind. The really quite amazing thing was, even though my body was under assault, it still functioned. It still had basic life needs, was still hungry, and tired, and restless. Just like any normal body. How was that possible?

Nurses, aides and doctors came and went in my room, day and night. I fast concluded this regular interruption was a necessary part of staying in a hospital. It's as if you're not getting your money's worth if you're not routinely interrupted. Apparently, checking your "vitals" is vital, usually on an every other hour schedule. Just when you're getting back to sleep from your last interruption, that's

---

1. Charles Wesley "Love Divine, All Loves Excelling," in *The Presbyterian Hymnal* (Louisville: Westminster John Knox, 1990) hymn 339.

the favorite time for a nurse to make sure you're, as Data from Star Trek would say, "Operating within normal parameters."

One evening, Steve was sitting in my room with me while I slept. Steve is many things—funny, handsome, smart, a techno-wizard. He is curious about most things. Steve watched all of the machines reporting their reports: my blood pressure, the oxygen level in my blood, my heart rate.

One time when I woke, he said, "it's really interesting what your heart rate does when someone comes in the room. It immediately starts beating faster, even when you're asleep. But when Greg walks in, it doesn't. Your heart seems to know the difference between Greg and everyone else."

Johnny was not just one handsome neurosurgeon. He also seemed to be a top dog at OHSU. One thing I wanted was to have a private room. But the population at the hospital was booming, and private rooms were the stuff of fairy tales. Still, he was able to pull it off. He found me a room each day that was mine alone. It did mean that I was a bit of a wanderer. One night in Adult Oncology, the next in the sterile ward for those with lymphoma. A third on the General Surgery floor. And then back to Adult Oncology. The day I was moved from Intensive Care to a regular room, my family surprised me by unwrapping a banner that was over eight feet long, its big block letters announcing HOPE & PROSPERITY.

I asked Ron years later, to remind me what he meant by these words, and he wrote:

> The context of the thought came from my work with the Cambodian community doing a commissioned Girl Scout video on how to make Girl Scouts acceptable to their culture and values. Girl Scouts being "fun" was not a high priority for Cambodians, "prosperity" was. They titled the video "Prosper My Daughter," an excellent cross culture work. From there I found the Latin word root for Hope was Spero or Spiro, and a Latin phrase "dum spiro," while I breathe, I hope; and so to hope for, to look and expect a good thing. Prosperity then from

a biblical POV seemed to embrace more than "money"
and wealth but a move towards hope as in Romans 5:1ff:
suffering, endurance, character, hope does not disap-
point us, because God's love has been poured into our
hearts through the Holy Spirit. So from there I saw your
life together as "pro-spiritus" or pro-sperity. I still do!

Each block letter of that banner was filled in with a different,
colorful design. The folks who had spent my surgery day at the
hospital worked on it and signed it with their prayers and wishes
for me. "I love you, Julie. Let's go to the beach. Greg." "Our prayers
are with you, love Pam, David, Matthew and Lara." "Grace and
peace to you, Julie. Ron Pierre Vignec." HOPE & PROSPERITY. I
do not know, now, how many hours I contemplated those words,
in the hospital and at home, hanging for months on our living
room wall. These words were utterly incompatible with my brain
tumor. They could not, with any integrity, inhabit the same room
where the news continued to be bad. Yet there they were. Bold and
unflinching, as if there was no question.

The colorful presence of these words led me to one way of
understanding, and thus negotiating, this crisis. I began to realize I
might not live through this, and I had to ask, what was finally true
for me? What was the final answer about my life? And I thought
about baptism.

When I perform a baptism, I involve the children in the congregation. I invite them up front and begin with a question: What's
the difference between a promise and maybe?

"A promise means it's gonna happen!" someone will offer. "It
means you're telling me the truth!" another shouts.

Even the littlest ones will nod their heads. They know the difference between "maybe" and "I promise." "I promise" is a done deal.
Money in the bank. They can go get their baseball mitts because
they're headed to the park. Whereas a maybe can't be trusted.

And then I tell them that at baptism God is making a promise
to the baby. God marks the baby as God's own. God promises to
love and care and watch over that baby, to help her grow up to be

strong and loved because she's now a part of God's treasured family. And the congregation is also making a promise to bring the baby up in the family of the church. Then I tell them to listen carefully for the promises made in the prayers during the baptism.

I was baptized and because I was baptized, my life has a promise that can't be killed by scans, tests, surgeries and chemicals. "In life and in death we belong to God." It is the beginning of the most recent confession of faith in the Presbyterian Church. In life and in death we belong to God. This simple truth was my shelter in the storm, reminding me there were truths about my life that remained true, no matter what. No matter what doctors told me. No matter what scans declared. No matter the results of poking and testing.

A week after the craniotomy, the pathology report finally came back. Johnny had told Greg the report, and as I found out years later, it was so bad that Greg had told no one for two days. He held in the devastating news because he didn't know how he was going to break it to me. One morning, Greg, Ron and Johnny came into my room together. I watched as they entered and thought, "this can't be good." They looked way too serious.

Greg and Ron grabbed my hands. I realized they'd planned every detail of this moment. I knew that they were trying to help me in any way they could. *Grab those hands, Julie. Hang on. They love you.*

Johnny said, "We've figured out what kind of tumor you have. It is a pinealblastoma. It's extremely rare and extremely malignant."

I held on tight to Ron and Greg's hands and nodded. My world began to spin.

I took a deep breath.

"O.K." I nodded my head. But it was not O.K. Not in the slightest.

What Johnny failed to mention, bless his heart, is that pineals are the most malignant, the fastest growing tumor, and they have grim survival rates. An article in the *National Library of Medicine* puts it this way: "Pinealblastomas, [primary tumors] which originate from the pineal gland, are extremely malignant tumors that grow quickly and aggressively. Because they spread so fast and the probability of long-term survival is poor, it is important to diagnose these tumors early."

Doctors Marie DeFrences and A. Julio Maritines explain it further in their discussion of pinealblastomas:

> Pinealblastomas are quite rare in adults. These neoplasms usually occur before age 20, are slightly more common in males and account for approximately 45% of pineal region tumors. Patients . . . commonly present with the signs and symptoms of obstructive hydrocephalus and/ or Parinaud's syndrome . . . [disorders that feature impairment of eye movement]. Therapeutic management of adults with pinealblastomas is controversial since few cases exist in the literature. A combination of radiotherapy and chemotherapy is usually attempted. Prognosis is dismal regardless of therapy regimen. One series of adults with pinealblastoma had a median survival of 30 months. Another series showed a 49% five-year survival following various treatment modalities.[2]

I felt cursed. Singled out to be a crash test dummy. Bad news was becoming inevitable news. I felt the universe was trying to break me.

When I was growing up, Steve tried it on occasion—break me, that is. We rarely fought, but we usually had one huge fight annually to make up for all the missing ones. One time he had me pinned face down on my parents' bed, my right arm twisted up against my back. "Say Uncle" he demanded and pushed my arm farther and

2. Marie DeFrences and Julio Martínez. "Final Diagnosis: Brain, Pineal Region, Stereotatic Biopsies: Pineoblastma," Case number 212. Online: http:// path.upmc.edu/cases/case212/dx.html/.

farther. I was determined not to give in. If he broke my arm, he broke my arm. If that happened, it would make this whole event much worse for him, and he knew it.

In a similar way, I felt now that the universe was pushing me to see just how far I'd go before I broke. Leave it to me to be hit with the most rare of tumors. And one of the most malignant. A pinealblastoma strikes only a handful of people throughout the country annually. Because there are so few incidents of pinealblastomas, there is a dearth of studies and survival rates related to different treatment modalities. When asked to consider the best treatment plan, it appears the scientific community offers a collective shrug, a "your-guess-is-as-good-as-mine" look on their bewildered faces.

Pinealblastoma. The beast had a name. But only that.

In the presence of this word, I heard only silence.

Then, a little girl broke through and reminded me that there were other places where words brought laughter and light.

> I suppose you are Mr. Matthew Cuthbert of Green Gables?" she said in a peculiarly clear, sweet voice. "I'm very glad to see you. I was beginning to be afraid you weren't coming for me and I was imagining all things that might have happened to prevent you. I had made up my mind that if you didn't come for me tonight I'd go down the track to that big wild cherry tree at the bend, and climb up into it to stay all night. I wouldn't be a bit afraid, and it would be lovely to sleep in a wild cherry tree all white with bloom in the moonshine, don't you think?"[3]

So begins *Anne of Green Gables*. I loved Anne from the start. She broke into my silent world with imagination and energy. My

3. L. M. Montgomery, *Anne of Green Gables* (London: Page, 1908, 1935) 11.

cousin sent me the book a few days after my craniotomy. The story begins when the orphan Anne comes, somewhat accidentally, to live with two aging siblings, Matthew and Marilla. Matthew and Marilla wanted to adopt a boy to help with the farm work, but instead, Anne was sent.

Anne's world was one of sunshine and imagination and surprises. When I felt overwhelmed with news that I could not take in, I asked someone to read to me from *Anne of Green Gables*. Her world was an entire star system away from mine. There I could breathe; there was nothing to fear at Green Gables.

Because my family was so devastated by the news, Johnny did some research. What he sought, miraculously, was right before him. A good friend and colleague of his at OHSU, Dr. Edward Neuwelt, had had good results with the few pinealblastomas he had treated.

Eight days after my craniotomy, my hospital room bright with morning sun, I sat with my head in bandages in a new robe Sylvia, Greg's mom, gave me. Dr. Neuwelt and his clinical coordinator, Annie Grummel, were coming to talk with me. Before they arrived, someone gave me a videotape about his program. It was called "Blood Brain Barrier Disruption."

An article in a nursing journal describes the Blood Brain Barrier program:

> The blood-brain barrier is made up of tight junctions which line the central nervous system capillaries. These tight junctions effectively exclude substances that are lipid insoluble and those of a molecular weight greater than 180 daltons. The molecular weight of most chemotherapy agents is between 200 and 1200 daltons. Therefore, most of the currently available therapeutic agents for the treatment of malignant brain tumors are unable to cross the barrier. This creates a discouraging clinical dilemma, particularly since the incidence of malignant brain tumors in the United Sates is rapidly

increasing. Currently, approximately 17,000 individuals are annually diagnosed with a brain tumor.

The technique [of opening the barrier] pioneered by Dr. Edward Neuwelt and the collaborators at Oregon Healthy Sciences University, involves an osmotic process. When capillary endothelial cells are exposed to a hyperosmolar solution, the cells shrink secondary to osmosis. This shrinkage places stress on the tight junctions which line the capillaries. With the stress, the tight junctions are pulled apart. This is the period of time when the blood-brain barrier is considered "open." [during this open period, chemotherapy agents are administered] This opening of the barrier is transient and reversible. Transient, since the blood-brain barrier normally provides a protective role by excluding toxic substances from the brain, and reversible because ideally the barrier should return to a normal baseline and be susceptible to osmotic opening again and again.[4]

This breaking up of the blood-brain barrier is called a disruption. To have a disruption, the patient is put entirely to sleep and a catheter is threaded to the brain along one of the brain's major arteries. A nondigestible sugar water is inserted into the brain, causing the tightly packed brain cells to shrivel. This shrinking temporarily opens the barrier. While it is open, Dr. Neuwelt injects the chemotherapy agents, effectively delivering ten to one hundred times more than the amount of chemo in traditionally injected chemo.

The essence of Dr. Neuwelt's theory is surprisingly simple. However, theory is one thing; practice is another matter entirely. For the patient, a disruption lives up to its name. For a time, disruptions throw the patient off balance. A typical regimen admits a patient monthly for twelve months. For each admission, the patient will have two disruptions. In order to get the sugar water to the

4. Nancy Doolittle et al., "Blood-Brain barrier Disruption for the Treatment of Malignant Brain Tumors: The National Program," *Journal of Neuroscience Nursing* 2 (1998) 81–90.

blood-brain barrier, a catheter is threaded into one of the femoral arteries, as it would be when a patient is having an angiogram. It enters the brain through one of two internal carotid arteries or the vertebral artery. There are three circulatory systems in the brain, and because malignant tumors are a "full-brain disease," the staff rotates which artery it uses, dousing each system with chemotherapy. In order to do this, the patient is put completely to sleep. After each disruption the patient immediately has a CT scan to allow the staff to rate the effectiveness of the disruption, varying from "Nil" to "Excellent," depending upon the cells' response to the osmotic solution. The staff is aiming for a middle ground: enough of a disruption to get the job done, but not enough to cause neurological symptoms. Although transient, the symptoms of a disruption range from double vision, coordination problems, orientation problems to deep sleep. Usually sooner, but sometimes later, these problems right themselves. And although your body goes through hell with the chemo drugs, it is not a permanent destination.

Dr. Neuwelt walked into the room: a man of medium build with dark hair and eyes and a neat beard. A woman came with him—his clinical coordinator, Annie. They both wore white doctor coats over their clothes. Annie had a stethoscope around her neck. She smiled easily; she seemed to be about my age. She was an expert at small talk, and as I watched her put my parents at ease with her casual questions, I thought, in a different situation we could've been friends.

Someone had given me a heads up that Dr. Neuwelt was coming to see if I was interested in being treated by him. I had a choice? This confused me when he hunkered in a chair at the end of my bed. He looked like a man playing poker; his face revealed nothing. In contrast to Johnny, who had the casual, joking manner of a late-night TV host, Dr. Neuwelt was all business. I have a distinct sense Dr. Neuwelt takes brain tumors as a personal offense: he is so driven to get rid of them. Maybe he knew he'd never be elected Mr. Congeniality, and so brought Annie with him when he talked with patients. Dear, sweet Annie. Her compassion balanced his brusque bedside manner. I don't think she ever lied to me, but somehow her calm words countered the fear Dr. Neuwelt often incited.

That first morning, I tried in my confused, somewhat blurry thoughts, to ask questions and get information. What I understood was that I had a choice between his method of treatment and the more traditional treatment of chemotherapy and radiation. A third option, I suppose, was no treatment at all. He explained that traditional treatment had a dreary prognosis. His program didn't offer solid ground for hope, but it was better than anything else I'd heard.

Then, in his typical, utterly realistic way, he said, "This is an extremely aggressive tumor. I can make it go away, but I don't know if I can keep it away."

"An extremely aggressive tumor." How many times did he say that to me over the next year? Looking back, I wonder if he worried that somehow I wasn't taking this brain tumor seriously enough. That first morning my thought, although I didn't say it, was to take it one step at a time. The obvious first step was to make it go away. Then we would take the next step. It was so simple. Take the most aggressive action to get rid of this.

When you are desperate, it's easy to commit yourself to that which you do not know.

When I agreed to join Dr. Neuwelt's program, the first thing he did was to order an MRI of my spine.

Pinealblastomas are nasty tumors, hell-bent on destroying their hosts. Not only do they grow fast, but they also delegate. They "seed," or send out cells to start other tumors in the cerebral spinal fluid. No one knew what, if anything, was in my spine. When Dr. Neuwelt ordered a spinal MRI, I dreaded what we might discover. By this time, I'd begun to expect bad news; I seemed to have a particular knack for it.

My spinal MRI was scheduled for the evening. Steve came with me and brought along *Anne of Green Gables*. He stood next to the MRI machine and began to read to me. At first, I could faintly hear him. But soon, the knocking all but blocked out his voice. Still, he read. Shouting above the noise, most words no longer distinguishable, I could barely hear him, but he continued to shout.

MRIs take a long time, forty-five minutes to an hour. His voice became hoarse. I lay in that machine and clung to the sound of his shouts. *Hold on, Julie. This is the sound of love.* I found unexpected comfort in the foolish shouts of my brother.

In the midst of the fear and bad news, my brother's life bore witness to the good news of the gospel: love never dies. He dared to make a fool of himself for the sake of love. With his shouts, he declared that his love was stronger than fear. That he would walk wherever I must go.

After the MRI of my spine, I was terrified. The MRI lasted much longer than they had told me it would. The techs were defensive, explaining they had trouble getting clear pictures of the center of my spine, due, they said, to my heart's beating and the movement of my lungs. I could tell they were sidestepping something, and once back in my room, I demanded to talk with the doctor on call. One of the interns assured me that it was not out of the ordinary for them to take several pictures of one section. The doctors would come in the morning to explain what, if anything, they saw. Whatever he said, I trusted him enough to calm down.

The next morning, it wasn't clear to me what the scans meant. The doctors stood around, looking at my spine lit up on the wall, trying to tell me what we were looking at. "You have tumor there," one said. "Or there." The confusion wasn't cleared up when they left, and Annie explained they really weren't sure what they were looking at. Later, Dr. Neuwelt finally convinced me.

His usually somber face had a dark shadow that morning. I knew my questions made him uncomfortable. He didn't like them, and they sometimes angered him. That morning, he was more distant than usual. In a clear, insistent voice, he said, "You have a considerable amount of tumor in your spine."

I nodded my head and gritted my teeth. When I asked what his plan for treatment was, he explained the plan was still the same. The chemotherapy goes throughout the cerebral spinal fluid. It goes through the brain and down the spine. I was relieved to know they had no new additional forms of torture planned.

Tumor in my spine. It was too much. And remained so. It was as if I could focus on the fact that I had a tumor in my head. As big as that was, somehow I could get my mind around that—no pun intended. But that was all. There was no more room in my awareness to take in the tumor in my spine. It was too vague. Amorphous. The threat was undefined. Nonspecific.

Several of my friends found ways to travel my journey with me. Pam's way was to talk with me on the phone in the evenings. Each night we had the phone and each other. There was something of a slumber-party feel to those conversations. Maybe, in part, because she wasn't standing at my bed with the requisite concerned look on her face, and we could talk normally, which was against the rules of crises, hospitals, MRIs, tests. We also had an intimacy, the kind born of hiding under the blankets with a flashlight, whispering so the big people won't hear. I found comfort in those phone confidences. I would slowly work into telling her the news. Results of MRIs. What was next.

When I heard of the tumor in my spine I didn't tell her straightaway. It was too big. I knew she would be devastated. I remembered one time she told me of a friend who was diagnosed with cancer in his spine, how he'd lived only a few months past that diagnosis. The implication: spinal cancer was fatal. Remembering her friend, I was afraid she would give up, stop believing that I could make it. If that happened, I didn't know how I would make it. When I told her, she held back her fears. Bless her.

The word became flesh: "I have tumor in my spine."

5

᙭

Wrestling at the River

And Jacob was left alone—
and a man wrestled with him until the breaking of the day.

Genesis 32:24

"DISCHARGE ME, Johnny. I want to go home."

It was the middle of the week. I was scheduled to come back Monday for my first disruption. I wanted some nights in my own bed. At home, no one could get me; I would be safe from needles and more bad news. Johnny cut me a deal, under-estimating my stubbornness.

"OK, Julie. If you can walk from here to that wall and back, you can go home."

On a good day I am not the most graceful of souls. The shower is a dangerous place for me. And I would not call that day, ten days after a craniotomy, a good day. With my poor brain still trying to adjust to the whole concept of being vertical, I looked to where he pointed. We were standing on the edge of a waiting room that felt ridiculously vast. Chairs and couches sat primly to our left. Waiting. There were windows to our right. At the moment, no one was doing any waiting in the waiting room. The wall to which he pointed was precariously, unreasonably far away, as if the designing architect had too much coffee the morning he designed that room and decided to make one of vast proportions. I stared at the brown wall and had absolutely no idea how I would make it. Stepping out, my feet protested when the floor began to sway and rock, a funhouse floor trying to throw me off balance. *I want to go home. I will not fall. I will not fall. Careful, Julie. Don't fall. I will not fall.* Like the little train that could, I started to move. I went slowly, hoping my steps looked graceful, in control. I held up my chin like a runway model, showing the latest in hospital attire. Turning was the hardest part; could I do it without falling?

I made it, barely, and learned a few things on that walk. The first, Johnny is a man of his word. He told Greg later, he never thought I'd make it. But I did, and he signed my discharge papers. Second, I had some say in determining how this battle would go. I did not will this disease, but I could fight it, and that will to fight would have its own power.

Monday morning came way too fast. Dr. Neuwelt was scheduled to leave town for a conference on Thursday and wanted to be present for my first two disruptions, so he scheduled them for Tuesday and Wednesday of that week. Because he was a crazy man about side-affects, he needed some baseline values—hearing, vision, IQ—before my first disruption. All of which is to say, Monday was an exhausting marathon of one test followed by another. My hearing was tested. My blood was tested. I had a Cat scan. I had a two-hour IQ test. The competitive part of me asked more than once how accurate the results could be, given that my brain had just operated on twelve days before.

This was followed by a convoluted passage to the Casey Eye Institute that was at the bottom of the Veteran's hospital, accessed by a vast transom hundreds of feet above the ground, providing stunning views of the OHSU campus and downtown Portland. The test was no regular eye test; rather it was a two-hour-long procedure, testing not only my vision and the overall health of my eyes but my peripheral vision as well. The machine to test peripheral vision was a large white oval with an indented screen and a cup for the testee's chin. It looked like a miss-shaped voting booth. I had to lean forward and plant my chin in the cup, and was told to blip a beeper every time I saw an indistinct flash somewhere in my circle of vision. To say that I was not in a great mood by this time wouldn't come close to how I was feeling. I was exhausted and wanted to scream to anyone within a hundred feet that I'd just had a craniotomy less than two weeks ago; apparently my wheelchair and head wraps weren't enough to tip folks off. I could've given a rip about a little flashing light. However, the tiny man who obviously thought this test was the most critical one in all the OHSU kingdom cut me no slack. He did not seem to get that I had a brain tumor. A brain tumor, for God's sake! Who cared about your little machine and its little flashes?

By the time Greg and I made our way back to my room on the floor of Adult Oncology, we were both exhausted. My roommate, Will, was a man who before he became a brain tumor patient had worked in the cancer research center at OHSU. He had a glioblastoma. Glios were the most common adult brain tumors; they were largely unresponsive to any known chemo agent. Still, his friends pooled their money together, with Dr. Neuwelt making up the difference, to pay for his treatment in an attempt to prolong his life as long as possible. His first disruption was to be at the same time as mine.

My parents, Steve, and Jody joined Greg and me, and we ate takeout Chinese in my cramped room. I had the bed by the window, so they sat on the windowsill while we tried in vain to find something to talk about. There's a reason hospital chatter is so utterly inane. It's because the big grey elephant stomping around the room is too out of control, too big, and too threatening to be the topic of polite conversation. To point to him and say, "Hey, look!" would be to open the door to fears that threatened all sense of normalcy and hope.

January 31, 1994, chart notes lay out the details:

> 30 y/o female recently c/o fatigue headache diplopia found by CT to have pineal mass and hydrocephalus. Underwent VP shunt Craniotomy [lead to] pineoblastoma.
>
> Patient to receive Carboplatin, Etoposide, Cytoxin. Etoposide and Cytox main side effects are bone marrow depression which at usual calculated doses allow spontaneous bone marrow recovery. Carboplatin produces bone marrow depression reversible but irreversible high frequency hearing loss.
>
> Arterial injury can also occur during catheter placement for chemo administration including femoral, carotid, vertebral arteries. The arterial injuries could range from minor to major permanent stroke or death. These occur infrequently but the chances are not zero. She seems to understand and wishes to proceed with B3D and chemo.

Face the threat of stroke, heart attack, or death. Or face an inevitable demise from a malignant brain tumor. Only someone with a death wish would call that a choice.

My family left. I put on my pajamas. Greg held me.

"I love you, Julie," he whispered in my ear. "I'll see you in the morning."

And he was gone.

In the morning I put on my hospital gown. My family came: Mom, Dad, Steve, Jody, and Greg. They walked me to the operating room but could go no farther. Greg kissed me one last time; and then as I lay on the gurney, the ultra wide doors swooped open and swallowed me. I entered a room crammed with machines, blinking lights, various tubes, IV poles with bags hanging on them. Three or four people stood around, their faces masked, their hands gloved. I had to "transfer" my body from the gurney to the operating table, as if it was something I wanted to do. Raymond, Annie's male counterpart, was there to help me.

I looked at him. I was suddenly overwhelmed by what I faced. Not just this one surgery, but twenty-four of them: two each month for twelve months. And this was just the first one. This was just the first day in 325 days.

"Oh, Raymond. How can I do this? This is just the first one."

"Yes," he said, holding my hand and looking me in the eyes. "But it is significant. You are beginning the fight."

He held on tight while the anesthesiologist put the mask over my face.

A few breaths. My head spun. And I was gone.

Walter Wangerin Jr., in *The Book of God*, describes Jacob's mysterious wrestling match this way:

> Jacob felt a wind, then a chill.
> Someone came flying down the riverbank. Jacob felt what he could not see. Then someone attacked him, struck him to the stony ground, and began to wrestle with him. They wrestled by the river. They whirled and heaved each other against the sheer rock wall.[1]

I am intrigued by this mysterious wrestling match. I wonder what went through Jacob's mind. He is on his way to make peace with his brother some twenty years after he had screwed him out of the family birthright. One could say this night wrestling match is his way of struggling with his guilt. Maybe. But somehow it feels more basic than that: like a life-and-death battle. The Hebrew

---

1. Walter Wangerin Jr., *The Book of God* (Grand Rapids: Zondervan, 1996) 67.

vayeyaveyk, "to wrestle," also means "to embrace." It's an intimate body encounter, legs and arms wrapped around one another. This battle took Jacob's entire concentration. It was a private, nightlong struggle between the two. Both of them giving their all to master the other.

I opened my eyes and saw a balloon—no, two balloons; wait, I'm wrong. It was one balloon, waving at the side of my bed. When I glanced around, I saw two of everything, as if I'd entered into "twin world." When I was little and had the-monster-is-chasing-me nightmares, if he was far enough away, I would sit down and close my eyes really, really tight, hoping I would wake up before the monster got me. In the hospital bed, I closed my eyes really, really tight, hoping to get back to a singular world, the place I was familiar with, where there was just one of everything.

Jody was sitting next to me.

"What time is it, Jod?"

"It's about seven-thirty."

"Yes, but morning or night?"

She couldn't hide her shock. "Night."

I had slept deeply after my initial disruption. The Cat scan they always performed after the barrier has been opened showed an "excellent" response to the disruption. In other words, my blood brain barrier responded too well to the disrupting agents. They would reduce the amount for the second one.

I lay on my back, not allowed to move because they had opened a main artery in my groin. To prevent blood clotting, leg massagers—a euphemism for mechanical plastic torture tubes—gradually squeezed my legs, starting from the ankle and working their way to just above my knees. It was like having a roving blood pressure cuff on my legs. And because I could not move, trips to the potty were entirely out of the question. I had a catheter to handle my urine. As they were flooding my body with water, my production of urine—how much, when—became the favorite topic for the nurses and doctors who looked in on me. Each ounce was studied carefully, measured and recorded in an ongoing journal.

The removal of both the leg squeezers and the catheter soon became my primary goal after each disruption. They were salt in the wound. Insult to injury. A metaphorical slap in the face. One more way to suffer in this torturous place. As if messing with my brain wasn't enough, these were like pesky mosquitoes whose main job was to make sure I didn't get too comfortable. Right. Like there was any chance of that.

My second disruption was a rerun of the first. Except the disruption was less disruptive. I woke up in the early afternoon, and by evening was able to actually take a walk down the hall. We went home the following day.

The walk down the hall became a goal I set for myself after each disruption. As I think on that now, what a stupid thing to do. Why not stay in bed, wallow in self-pity and have people wait on me hand and foot? Why not milk this baby for all it's worth and get as much attention and spoiling as possible? But along with waiting until the morning to put on my hospital gown, walking became a ritual. It was one way I fought what was happening. One way to say that I was still there. Still strong. My body wasn't totally beaten. Not yet.

Jacob's night struggle is a good image for the singular battle I fought. In my journal, dated September 19, 1994, I wrote:

> Fighting the tumor remains the most focused struggle of my life. While it is true, I really do believe I would not have made it were it not for the prayers, gifts, visits— love's tangibles—it is also completely clear that it was only me in the wheelchair, on the gurney. A future was at stake for all of us: would I be here next year? But the future at stake was, at its very core, my future. I watched with tired amazement how the world continued to

function. On the freeway, cars raced by, going to work. To shop. Whatever.

Even those who made it their business to be with me in the hospital couldn't (nor should they) hide the difference. Colleen brought Michael by in his little elf Halloween costume. Catherine stopped by after work to say hello. Peggy visited with little gifts and warm grace. Mom and Dad came every month, with flowers or a present from Nordstrom. Colleen sent the luxurious treat of fresh fruit . . .

All the while, I was in the hospital bed. My family would go to the cafeteria for lunch. Or out for dinner. I finally asked those who came early in the morning to see me off, drinking coffee and eating scones, to leave their breakfasts until I was in surgery. The aroma, the sips, were too much. Too much for my empty, growling stomach. Too much for my heart, which saw in those steaming cups the essential, fundamental chasm between me and the rest. Coffee and scones. Life those mornings was normal for them in a way it would not be for me.

There were two moments, two times during each of my monthly treatments, that were the hardest for me. These moments made it transparent the battle was singly mine. I was alone in the shadows.

One was the first night of each stay. Greg stayed with me late into the night. He helped me get into my pj's and gently he said goodnight. The lights dimmed. I watched Letterman, waiting for the Phenobarbital to take effect. While Dave skewered his latest victim and the audience laughed in the background, I gritted my teeth, wrapped my arms tightly around the nothingness, and held on for dear life.

The second hardest moment was arriving at the doors of the operating room, the end of the slippery slope into patienthood. This time, I did the leaving. Mom, Dad, Steve, and Greg . . . they came with me to those doors but could go no farther. I hated those wide doors, lobster claws swooping out, opening up to take me in. I hated saying goodbye, kissing Greg, squeezing Dad's hand. Making promises I wanted so badly to keep. "See you this afternoon."

"In a breathless silence they wrestled all night . . . until a high grey dawn began to streak the sky." A breathless silence. Why did Wangerin see it that way? They could've easily been screaming and grunting. The Bible doesn't give us any help. My hunch is, Wangerin must know something of the shadow valley to imagine it so.

The riverbank is stunningly silent. When you struggle for your life, there are no words to describe this essential striving. The author of Jacob's story gives us no explanation for the attack. Neither is Jacob's attacker justified in any way. The man jumps him when he is alone, beside the river. It is a place of no-word, only a speechless, threatening stranger.

The tumor slammed my life to the ground, forcing me to focus solely on one question: will I live? For an answer there was no word. Only silence.

Frederick Buechner describes such a silent moment in his *Telling the Truth: The Gospel as Tragedy, Comedy, and Fairy Tale.* He writes of a man who wants to know the truth. He is Pontius Pilate, and Jesus is standing before him.

> The man stands in front of the desk with his hands tied behind his back. You can see that he has been roughed up a little. His upper lip is absurdly puffed out and one eye is swollen shut . . .
>
> "So, you're the king of the Jews," he says. "The head Jew," because there hasn't been one of them yet who hasn't made this his claim.
>
> The man says, "It's not this world I'm king of," but his accent is so thick that Pilate hardly gets it, the accent together with what they have done to his upper lip. As if he has a mouth full of stones, he says, "I've come

> to bear witness to the truth," and at that the procurator of Judea takes such a deep drag on his filter tip that his head swims and for a moment he's afraid he may faint.
>
> He pushes back from the desk and crosses his legs . . . Standing by the door, the guards aren't paying much attention. One of them is picking his nose, the other staring up at the ceiling . . . Pilate squints at the man through the smoke and asks his question.
>
> He asks it half because he would give as much as even his life to hear the answer and half because he believes there is no answer . . .
>
> He says, "What is truth?" and by way of an answer, the man with the split lip doesn't say a blessed thing.[2]

Certainly my question lacked Pilate's hazy curiosity, and was much more specific. I desperately needed to know the answer to the questions, what is true? Will I live? For a definitive answer, I didn't hear a blessed thing. So, the debate raged. Did I have solid ground to hope? Or was I simply deluding myself that I could beat this thing? Were there any rational reasons, any past experiences with pinealblastomas that suggested the possibility that someone could survive this? Or did I need to rely solely on my will to live, my stubbornness to get through this? That and the prayers of my friends?

The question was constant. It became part of the air I breathed. Even when I wasn't entirely focused on it, able at times to think of other things, still, it twisted and wrestled somewhere in me. I looked around in my world, seeking any clues. I searched people's eyes, listened for the tone they used to talk to me about my brain tumor. Did he flinch? Did she look away? Do they know more than they are telling? Are they only trying to protect me from the truth?

Most of the time this wrestling took place in the halls of science. Dr. Neuwelt would insist, "This is an extremely aggressive tumor." Annie would say later, "Yes, but it is also very responsive to chemotherapy."

2. Frederick Buechner, *Telling the Truth: The Gospel as Tragedy, Comedy, and Fairy Tale* (San Francisco: Harper & Row, 1977) 12–14.

After talking with Annie, Steve put the two together. Chemotherapy is most effective on dividing cells. If you have a fast-growing tumor, you have a lot of dividing cells. Thus, chemo is dramatically effective. Is it good news that my tumor typically responds? Or is it bad news that the reason it responds is because it grows so fast? Never an answer, always a doubt. The arguments thrashed about in my head.

The second time I was admitted for a disruption, they did a CT scan to see if the first round of chemo had had any effect. Early the next morning, before surgery, Dr. Neuwelt made rounds to tell us the results of the scan. Lord knows, by this time I was ready for a little good news. Did the tumor respond to the first round of chemo? I knew the results of the scan would be another voice jumping into the struggle. But the tumor wasn't playing. There had been no change. It hadn't grown—the good news. But neither had it shrunk—bad news? Certainly not great news. We had yet to make any strides towards killing it. But, Annie told us, there is often no visible change after the first round.

There were times when my questions retreated to the background; they weren't always right before me, and I would be able to find some balance while quietly going about my days, one step at a time. But, out of the blue, I could be slammed again. Thrown off balance. Typically, I was looking the other way, not expecting the attack. It almost felt as if the enemy was taking on a personality, watching to make sure I didn't get too comfortable, insisting I take the tumor with all seriousness.

This happened one time at the beach. I have gone to Manzanita, this little Oregon coastal town, all my life. It is a sleepy beach town with a vast windy stretch of beach. The main street is all of five blocks, perpendicular to the ocean. When I was growing up, my grandparents owned a little house a half block from the beach. I would fall asleep to the never-ending sound of waves crashing to shore.

When I was a kid and we'd go to the beach, my dad and my grandfather would make the usual crabbing trip, and if the season was right, they would come back with buckets of live crab. Then Mom and Dad would take a huge pot down to the beach, swoop up some ocean water, haul it back to the house and put it on the stove. Meanwhile, some torturing soul would let the live crabs totter on the grass with our German Shepherd, Dagmar, jumping at them barking and hopping back to avoid their claws. When the windows of the cabin were steamed up and the water was boiling, Dad would pick up a live crab and drop it unceremoniously into the steaming water. I watched in horror as the crab's claws reached for the sky, and swore that I could hear it scream.

To confirm that I was raised by a barbarian clan that somehow reincarnated themselves into the twentieth century, I sat in the other room and watched my "family" hunched over a table, holding freshly cooked, bright-red crab legs dipped in melted butter to their drooling mouths. No need for civility at this point. They ripped the legs apart with their fingers and teeth and made moaning sounds that I would later associate with sex and eating really good chocolate. When they were done, sucking their lips and licking their fingers, my brother would look my way, perplexed at the look of disgust on my face, and say, "an Anderson who doesn't like crab? That's impossible. They must've mixed up the babies in the nursery."

We made it a point to go the beach on July Fourth, when this little town put on one great fireworks show. Steve and I would spend all day building a fort with driftwood. Later, we would build a great fire and cuddle in wool blankets to watch the show. I can't think about those times without remembering one summer when Dagmar was with us. Dagmar was terrified of the noise, so we left her at the house with my grandma, who stayed behind to watch from the window. Our great big dog spent the evening quivering in my poor grandmother's lap.

By the summer of my tumor, the town had grown up a bit. There were a few more places to eat, and a little store that sold local art. There was also a swanky bed and breakfast, built on the main street, skillfully hidden among the trees, along with a hotel that has been there since the dawn of time.

Greg and I went with two of our best friends from Princeton, Hunter and Susan. Hunter and Susan lived in Charlotte, North Carolina, and had never been to Oregon. When I was first in the hospital, Dad promised me a trip to the beach; I took him up on it, and we rented a house on a cliff with a fantastic view of the ocean. Susan suffers from alopecia and so wears a wig. How wonderful to have a sister in baldness. This did, however, create a challenge when we walked on the windy beach.

Susan and I went to town to have our nails done, a nice way to spoil yourself when you didn't have hair that needed cutting, Susan pointed out. It was the town's one little beauty parlor, a small blue duplex shared with a realtor. Susan had her nails done first and went back to our cabin. A kind woman somewhere in her sixties was chatting with me while she filed my nails.

As she massaged my hands, I felt safe. According to hospital rules, I was not supposed to have my nails painted before a disruption so I asked for a French manicure, which is one where white is painted at the end of your nails, with pink on the rest. The manicure was beautiful, but also looked very natural. I assumed I could sneak those manicured hands into the hospital without being found out. With my wig, I could pretend to be normal, even healthy. It was an expensive wig, and looked very much like real hair.

I enjoyed fading back into the world. I could forget needles and hospitals and drugs for a while and simply enjoy life.

The manicurist began to talk about her daughter. When she spoke, her eyes gazed off into the distance. I thought her daughter must not live close by.

I asked her where her daughter lived.

She stopped for a minute, holding my fingers in her hand. Looking up and out the window, far away.

"She used to live in Seattle. But she's not alive now. She died of a brain tumor." Taking a small breath, a brief pause, she turned back to my nails. In a chatty tone, she explained, "It hit her fast. We had no time to treat it. One week she wasn't feeling well, and two months later she was dead."

I held my breath.

I looked in her eyes. "How awful. I'm so sorry."

It took all my concentration to keep from crying. I asked a few questions. I wanted to show her compassion and sympathy, as any stranger would. All the while, a voice sneered, "See? See there? There's a woman about your age who didn't make it. Someone just like you. You want an answer to your question? You just got it."

I focused on the nail file, I focused on the table before me and the rhythm of the woman's voice. I told myself that what was true for her daughter was not necessarily what would be true for me. Death by brain tumor was another woman's story, not mine. Still, when Greg picked me up, I got into the car and sobbed. What are the chances? This woman could've just as easily been a grandmother, bragging about her grandkids. Or she could've lost her daughter in a plane crash. Or I could've had someone else do my nails. What powers moved to create such a horrific coincidence—that here, in this tiny town, in an out-of-the-way beauty shop, I would run into a woman who had lost a daughter to a brain tumor?

Another time I was slammed to the ground was at the hospital. I'd been through a handful of treatments. The tumor was starting to shrink. I was beginning to settle into the routine of disruptions—an ironic phrase; how can "disruptions" be routine? The program had a few nurses whose specialty was to care for disruption patients. There were two disruption patients to one room, and one nurse provided constant, eight-hour care for us. My first few disruptions, MJ was my nurse. She was attentive, thoughtful, and kind, always sitting near the end of my bed. We talked often, when I was conscious. But we never talked about the nature of my tumor.

One month I had a different nurse, Andy. One evening after a disruption, she and I were talking and she began to explain the different categories of brain tumors treated in the disruption program.

"There are some that we really can't do anything for. There are others that we can pretty much cure. Then there are those, like yours, where we can't cure, but are buying you time. We can slow it down, but we can't get rid of it."

Andy sounded so sure, I was inconsolable. I felt she was the only one telling me like it was. Up to that point I wondered if maybe people were unwilling to come clean, to tell me the truth. But Andy just had. And my fear exploded with a voice, screaming, "Everyone is sugarcoating the truth. No one is willing to tell you the real deal. But Andy just told you the real deal." Any faint hope I put in recent scans that showed the tumor shrinking immediately vanished with her words.

I later told Annie what Andy had said. Annie was furious, declaring that no one knew what the outcome would be, not even Dr. Neuwelt. Andy had been completely out of line to say that to me.

I so wanted to believe Annie's apology, but the damage was significant.

It wasn't all bad news. Other voices joined the struggle. They came to give me strength in the wrestling match. In unexpected ways, clearly. They had their own power.

One sunny spring day during my treatments Greg and I were in Seattle visiting my parents, when my friend Steve Wilhelm came to visit. I'd met Steve the year after I graduated from college; we worked together on a little trade journal in Seattle and had kept in touch since. He was on a spiritual journey quite different from mine, exploring Eastern religions, and was a committed, practicing Buddhist. His brown eyes were deep pools of calm, reflecting years of meditative practice. Steve was curious about Jesus and always interested in talking with me about my own faith journey. Even though we didn't use the same faith vocabulary, we shared a strong connection. He once mused that maybe we were monks together in a previous life.

Greg and I went on a long walk with Steve. There was a forested trail in a greenbelt not far from my parents' house. It was an easy path that wound around tall cedar and Douglas fir trees. The sun sparkled through their branches. It was the first time he'd spent time with Greg, and he asked Greg how it was for him. The three of us had an honest, hopeful conversation about the shadow valley. We came back and sat on the deck of my parents' home for iced tea.

"I'm no doctor," Steve said, "but I think you're going to make it. I sense this white light around you. Listening to your stories, how your friends and family are with you . . . I don't know. I just think you're going to make it."

Deep within me I felt a confirmation, a strong certainty that I would live. I heard a new voice, "It's true; you will survive this." I felt like a child on Christmas morning, just about to open my presents. I was excited, thrilled, and grateful all at once; no doubt Santa knew exactly what I wanted and some things I didn't know I wanted. Those moments were a warm blanket to calm my shivering fears. I looked those fears square in the eye. *Did you hear that? You're wrong! I'm getting through this.*

Life's certainty came to me in other ways. Dr. Bentson, a bit mystified, told me of a dream she had right after we discovered my tumor. She saw me wearing a hearing aid, and limping with a cane. She understood that to mean I would survive. I understood the hearing aid but worried the cane meant I would become disabled. Dr. Bentsen suggested the cane might have been a symbol of old age. I decided that was my story, and I was sticking to it.

Annie offered words of hope too. Each time I was admitted, she'd exclaim how great I looked. I had energy and passed each neurological exam with flying colors.

The summer of '94 I went to a writing conference at Vancouver School of Theology led by Madeleine L'Engle, one of my favorite authors. My small group there gathered me up in prayer, giving me tremendous strength.

So it went—back and forth. Some days I knew I would live. Others I had to wrestle with words and images that told me I would not. With little help from vague explanations and inconclusive scans, I struggled to answer the essential question: Would I live?

It was an uncertainty that we all battled, as we tried to find any sliver of hope, any light filtering through the darkness.

My journal entry:

June 6, 1994

I am supposed to be at the hospital today. But instead of my white blood cell count climbing, like I thought, it's gone down again. Not even close to what it needs to be—and low enough that I can't go out—again—must be home . . . And I wonder why my body is so reactive—so non-cooperative—so unpredictable. And I hate that this is happening to me, that I have very little control over even how I will spend my days.

We got back from Seattle and visiting Mom and Dad Saturday. It was a nice visit—and the first time Dad has seen me vertical and healthy since January. He has only seen me in the hospital—that can't be good for him.

When I was three years old, we lived in a cul-de-sac. I was talking with the neighborhood kids when I leaned back against the neighbor's car, my hands behind me, resting against the headlight. The headlight was cracked and cut my hand, right at the base of my pinky-finger. Confused and horrified at the blood, I ran home to Mom, knowing that she would be able to calm me and make it better.

Last weekend, that image kept coming back to me. I so want to go to her and ask her: "What is this thing that is happening to me? Please help me understand it and make it better." But this is not a cut finger, this is a brain tumor—mysterious, hidden, life-threatening. And though it's making her crazy, Mom can't make it better. And so many little things tell me that it's all she can do to function. I can't bring this question to her.

And God? What of God? Why would God stand by to watch this enemy attack me by the river?

My friend Steve once wrote me about the dog he and his wife adopted.

He had an ear infection, so I had to put drops in it. You
know, it was really hard because he didn't get what was
going on. And there's really no way to tell him, right?
And after, he shot me this look and ran out of the room
with his tail between his legs. A couple of hours later, he
slowly came back into the room and hid under a side
table. He glared at me with this look, like "I thought you
were my friend." You know there was this kind of disillusionment that happened. And I couldn't do anything
to help him understand.

I am not implying any parallel between the ear infection of a
dog and a brain tumor. But I do understand the disillusionment,
when one you've trusted allows something unimaginable to happen
to you. I wasn't angry at God, but I was mystified. My admittedly
narcissistic image of a loving God who only brought good things
to me, and kept all the bad things away, no longer held. Confused
and stunned, I no longer knew how to think about God.

Nicholas Wolterstorff is a philosophical theologian who lost
his twenty-five-year-old son in a rock-climbing accident. In his
book, *Lament for a Son*, he writes:

I am at a loss. I have read the theodicies produced to
justify the ways of God to man. I find them unconvinc-
ing. To the most agonized question I have ever asked I
do not know the answer. I do not know why God would
watch him fall. I do not know why God would watch me
wounded. I cannot even guess.

I am not angry but baffled and hurt. My wound is an
unanswered question. The wounds of all humanity are
an unanswered question.[3]

An unanswered question breaks you. All preconceived no-
tions no longer hold. It is a hurricane ripping away all that is not
nailed down. A wind that whips your house to shreds, leaving only
the fireplace and an old shoe. A necktie hanging from a tree.

My tumor was an unanswered question.

3. Nicholas Wolterstorff, *Lament for a Son* (Grand Rapids, MI: 1987) 68.

6

❧

Winter

Let us remember that the life in which we ought to be interested is
"daily life." We can, each of us, only call the present time our own.[1]

—St. Gregory of Nyssa

Oh, I've had my moments, and if I had to do it over again,
I'd have more of them. In fact, I'd try to have nothing else.
Just moments, one after another, instead of living so many
years ahead of each day.[2]

—Nadine Stair, eighty-five years old, Louisville, Kentucky

*T*HERE YOU are. *You're showing yourself.* I was facing the mirror
in our little bathroom, looking into my eyes. One pupil was

1. Gregory of Nyssa, "On the Lords' Prayer" in Kathleen Norris: *The Quotid-*
ian Mysteries: Laundry, Liturgy and Women's Work (New York: Paulist, 1988)
introduction.

2. Nadine Stair in Jon Kabat Zin's *Full Catastrophe Living: Using the Wisdom*
of Your Body and Mind to Face Stress, Pain, and Illness (New York: Dell, 1990) 17.

large, the other much smaller. Mom noticed the difference our second day home from the hospital and called Annie. Annie told us this disparity is common with pinealblastomas. I looked into my eyes and saw my enemy staring back.

Like my tumor, winter stripped away any pretense. It was cold that January. Brutally so. And piercingly clear. The sun, low on the horizon, bounced off the pavement, the leaves of grass, the river flowing through town. Blinding and brilliant. The trees were bare, their branches quivering in the cold, their bare arms raised pleadingly. The sky was a crisp, deep, bright blue, intense.

Somehow, the extreme clarity of the very air I breathed fit with my experience. My days were intensely focused on one thing, staying alive. I breathed in the air, felt it enter my body, shivered with the chill of it. While I gave thanks that I was alive—thanks that for the moment my body functioned—I saw in the mirror the abnormality in my pupils and was struck by the fact that I could take nothing for granted.

Cancer is the winter of the soul. It strips life to its roots, making a life's landscape barren. Serious illness takes away all of the false suppositions upon which we've built our lives. No way to hide in the daily lists of things to do. No way to pretend my life was full because I was busy doing my job or cleaning the house, or playing. My life was reduced to the steel cold truth that I had a brain tumor. I faced two eyes with unequal pupils looking back from the mirror and bearing witness to what we could not see.

Severe illness is a profound shock to the system. It dislodges you. You look in the mirror and one of the unfortunate ill stares back.

Mark Ian Barasch, a thirty-year practitioner of Buddhism and author of three books exploring the various aspects of healing, writes:

> You could say that disease also abrades away, painfully, all of these superficial ways in which we judge our worthiness, even life's worthiness. Our worthiness as in: "Am

I strong, beautiful, competent, undamaged goods?" Or,
life's worthiness as in: "Life is good only when it makes
me happy, or aggrandizes me, or favors my enterprise."[3]

When I was healthy, I would rush out the door to meet someone for coffee or begin my research for an upcoming sermon or
attend a staff meeting or sit with a parishioner in the hospital. But
home from my hospital stays, I woke when I woke, took my various pills, had fresh fruit for breakfast. My days were slow and they
gave the time to wade through the cards that came, write thank-
you notes for the flowers and meals that flowed from the river of
concern and care from the church and our friends. We had put
up the "Hope and Prosperity" poster along one wall of the living
room. The wall became a vast bulletin board, and we taped my
favorite cards underneath it. My mom told one of the attorneys in
her office that his card made it on the wall, and he was visibly flat-
tered! "Really?" he asked. Flower bouquets took over one corner
of our living room, creating a small jungle. Greg took me on little
walks around our neighborhood. I slept.

All the while, I paid attention to my body. Was I dizzy?
Hungry? There were intense headaches if I stayed vertical too
long. The back part of my skull was missing. "You don't need that
anyway," Johnny quipped, to which I responded, "If I don't need
it, why did I have it in the first place?" It was as if the very plates
that made up my skull were shifting, trying to figure out a new way
to join now that one part was missing. When I described this to
Annie, she told me that was exactly what was happening.

The church was terrifically supportive, not only with cards,
but with meals. They set up a schedule, and for several months
someone delivered dinner each night. They also kept in touch, with
cards and letters.

One man, Jim, sent occasional letters. This letter was written
February 2, 1994.

3. Mark Ian Barash in Derrick Jensen's, "Body Language: A Conversation
with Mark Ian Barasch on Illness and Healing," *The Sun* (Chapel Hill, NC: The
Sun Publishing Co. Inc., January 2000, issue # 289) 5,6.

Dear Greg and Julie,

Your letter to the congregation was very upbeat. I needed that. I liked your clever brain surgery disclaimer and your comment about meal strategy.

After Johanna read your letter, I suspect Aline and I weren't the only ones with lumpy throats.

I had a dream that we were gathered up front as if to serve communion. We ascended some steps behind the pulpit, (Anglican Church-type) descend some steps, and you are lying on a step in your minister's robe, I step over you and say, "Hi." You respond with a cheerful, "Hi."

Well I suppose Freud could write a chapter or 2 on that one.

I attended the Synod Insurance meeting in Millbrae Jan. 22nd. We went around the table introducing ourselves and I told them you had just had surgery and that we were very concerned about it. After the meeting, I visited briefly with Ed Danzig who made the presentation. He remembered talking to you about an "incident," and he was impressed with the way you handled it!

I'm looking forward to Johanna reading another Epistle from you.

> Cheers,
> Jim
> FAN CLUB MEMBER

Arthur Hoppe was a San Francisco journalist and columnist for fifty years, and in the *San Francisco Chronicle* on January 17, 2000, he wrote of living with his recent diagnosis of lung cancer.

No one ever has a good thing to say about cancer. Mention the disease and people turn up their collars and shudder. It's high time someone listed a few of its benefits. Call me the Pollyanna to end all Pollyannas, if you will, but I'll give it a try.

First of all, it wins you letters and calls from friends you haven't seen for years. My children phone regularly, and my dear wife of more than 50 years and I have never been closer . . .

> I sleep late, I nap, I read, I even type a little at home,
> but only when I feel like it . . .
>
> The fact is I've become irresponsible. And having
> been bound up in responsibility all of my life, as most of
> us are, there's nothing as joyous as being irresponsible—
> as long as you have a good excuse.[4]

Before we discovered my tumor, Greg made a commitment to teach one day a week at Pacific Lutheran University in Tacoma, Washington. Ron wisely suggested he still do it; it would give him an experience that was normal in a way that our life clearly wasn't. Greg drove over three hours to get there, taught for three hours, then drove home the same day. It was a long, grueling day. When I was first home, we all thought it best if I had company on the days he was gone.

I remember two of those days vividly. They were like snow days. Growing up in the Pacific Northwest, I thought the occasional snowfall was the best thing ever. When I was a kid, the Seattle metro area must have had all of one snowplow with a bored guy named Joe sitting in front of his TV, waiting for the call to pull it out of the garage, dust it off, and save the city. Two or three flakes fell, and people went into crisis mode. Seattle had several bridges that always froze. Hills surrounded the metro area and cars slid around, driven by nervous, inexperienced motorists. It made some sense to get off the streets and go home. Did we have enough food to make it through? How's our supply of firewood? A snowfall of any intensity basically shut down the city. If enough fell, meaning if it stuck on the roads, it closed schools. The bus service was mostly shut down, too, making it impossible for Mom and Dad to get to work. Snow days were free days, a city-sanctified permission to be irresponsible. Snow days proved that, beside brain surgery, there are very few things that absolutely *had* to happen. It was a legitimate excuse to drop whatever you had to do and stay home and play.

4. Arthur Hoppe, "A Few Good Things to Say about Cancer," *San Francisco Chronicle*, January 17, 2000.

The first time Greg was gone, my brother Steve came to spend the day with me. When I was a kid, I adored it when he paid any attention to me. It didn't matter the game—Monopoly or double-solitaire. He was my wonderful big brother, and he was actually playing with me. How cool was that! We regularly watched *Star Trek* together—even back then, I thought Captain Kirk was handsome, though full of himself.

The day he spent with me we were as irresponsible, except for monitoring my medications, as we could be. We watched the winter Olympics. We ate when we felt like it. We laughed hysterically at almost everything. Growing up, we often found things to laugh about. Steve has a gift: he finds everyday people tremendously funny. Because I know my brother has little to no self-control, I waited until the afternoon to bring out the three-way popcorn bucket we'd been given for Christmas.

Steve's eyes got really big.

"Wow! It's a good thing you didn't bring that out earlier!" he said as he reached for his first handful of caramel corn. My impulse control was not a whole lot better than his; we ate way too much popcorn. I grossed him out with my carrot juice. We played Nerts, a fast-action card game where speed is everything. He razzed me about my crush on Tomba, the Italian downhill skier who kept the media's eyes on him by posing with beautiful women. We forgot the rest of the world for a day.

The second week Greg was gone, Pam decided to spend the day with me. I insisted I would be fine, but she didn't listen, and took that day off. I felt lucky that she would spend the entire day with me. We talked until our jaws hurt. We laughed. Her back hurt; she lay on the floor. We took naps. She tried hopelessly to balance my checkbook, a true measure of love if ever there was one. That afternoon we rented a video of *Anne of Green Gables* and laughed and cried.

That evening, when Greg wasn't home yet, she helped me get into bed. It was a complicated matter, as I slept with my head and back elevated with several pillows, and had a few pillows to lift my knees and ease my back pain.

"Can you believe this?" I laughed. "I'm practically barricaded in bed!"

"Yeah, but you know what? It's your bed." She sat on the side of it and held my hand.

"You're right." Pause.

"So, what do you think? Do you think I can beat this thing?" I looked into her eyes; she looked right back at me.

"With all of my heart, I hope that you can. And the news that fast-growing tumors respond well to chemo is really good. And I think you are in the very best program for your kind of tumor. I think we are very lucky that you found Dr. Neuwelt. I think God led you to him."

"So do I." A tear trickled down my cheek.

I remembered that Dr. Neuwelt explained that the treatments might cause some hearing impairment.

"I can't imagine what becoming hearing impaired will be like. But I don't think it will be that big of a deal; it's not too much of a price to pay for my life."

"You'd better get some sleep. I'll stay out in the living room until Greg gets home. He should be home soon." She kissed my cheek. "I love you, Julie."

"I love you too. Thanks for spending the day with me. I had a great time."

Both of those visits were a grace; I felt loved, spoiled, and very lucky.

At the bottom of it all, serious illness scratches away any illusions we carry about time. If there is always a tomorrow, then most everything in our lives can be penultimate. Important, but not critical. Lying in the hospital bed with a rare and fast-growing brain tumor, I no longer had Scarlett O'Hara's luxurious assumption that tomorrow will come. When Dr. Neuwelt came to meet me that first morning in the hospital, I guessed that there was a strong likelihood my tomorrows were numbered in the lower digits. Dr.

Neuwelt could not promise me twenty more years, but he could promise me a year or two. With a brain tumor, you take what you can get.

Jon Kabat-Zinn runs a stress-reduction clinic at the University of Massachusetts Medical Center, where he teaches patients the skill of meditating on the moment and how to practice mindfulness.

In the first chapter of his book, *Full Catastrophe Living*, Kabat-Zinn defines "mindfulness practice":

> Knowing what you are doing while you are doing it is the essence of mindfulness practice . . . there is nothing particularly unusual or mystical about meditating or being mindful. All it involves is paying attention to your experience from moment to moment. This leads directly to new ways of seeing and being in your life because the present moment, whenever it is recognized and honored, reveals a very special, indeed magical power: *it is the only time that any of us ever has.* The present is the only time that we have to know anything. It is the only time we have to perceive, to learn, to act, to change, to heal. That is why we value moment-to-moment awareness so highly . . . It makes our experiences more vivid and our lives more real.[5]

"In illness you're suddenly not yourself anymore," Marc Ian Barasch writes. I'm not sure that I agree. Life-threatening illness blows away all the external supports you've built up, all the ways of being that you relied on to define yourself. It is more precise to say you are suddenly not who you thought you were. The winter of my life did not destroy *me*. It forced me to look inward. I had to cut to the chase. In this place I did not choose, who was I? What in my life was meaningful?

---

5. Jon Kabat-Zinn, *Full Catastrophe Living* (New York: Delacorte, 1990) 28–29.

A brain tumor is a kind of crash course in Buddhism. You must live your life for the moment, because it is all you have.

There is a picture that sits on our mantle. Eight of us stand on the beach huddled together, bundled up in winter coats, hats, hoods. Catherine is there on the far right—her husband, Mark, takes up the other side of the group. Four of them are members of a pastor-support group I'd been a part of for over a year; the rest are spouses or friends. David and Johanna are there, smiling and holding their eight-month-old daughter. I am standing in the front row, right of center with a black hat and bangs. Greg is behind me, his arms wrapped around my waist. We're all smiles and look like any crazy group of Oregonians out to frolic in the bitter wonders of the winter coast.

But looks can be deceiving. This picture was taken in the winter of my illness. My pudgy cheeks were not so because I was so healthy, but because I was on steroids to shrink the tumor. My "bangs" were actually a strip of hair meant to give the illusion of hair under a hat, a poor woman's wig.

Greg had arranged this surprise gathering of friends. I thought we were going to spend the weekend, just the two of us. Although, to be honest, I had overheard some suspicious conversations on the phone he'd had the week before. And when we pulled up to the rental house, I saw several different footprints in the sand that led to the front door. When we opened the front door, I was greeted by the warm air of the cabin and several friends, all in their slippers, standing around with coffee and tea. "Surprise!" they yelled, lifting their mugs.

I kept my hat on—I didn't want to spoil the time with the distraction of my bald head. Frankly, I can't remember what we ate or the things we talked about, but I do know the conversations ranged from the mundane to the sublime.

And I remember that on Saturday, Mark, Catherine's husband, thought he'd try a little snorkeling. In the rough waves of the Oregon coast, in the stormy, bone-chilling cold waters. I love Mark—he is an adventurous kind of guy. And somewhat of an innocent at heart. He grew up in the Midwest, and at that time, he hadn't spent much time on the Oregon coast. As he walked down to the water in his wet suit, with his goggles and snorkel, I kept my fear in check but tried to say in an understated, nonnagging voice, "You know, Mark, the water's really, really cold. And I don't know about the winter undertows, they might be pretty fierce . . . " He didn't stay in the water long, and I don't know what he saw in its murky depths.

It was a weekend full of rich moments that told me how loved I was.

Greg's gift to me.

In his novel *Corelli's Mandolin*, Louis De Bernieres describes the thoughts of the Greek prime minister, Metaxis. The Second World War is heating up; Mussolini is rising to power. As Metaxis ponders what to do about Mussolini, he also contemplates his own death. His body is failing, and he knows, with a kind of detached and passive grief, that he will soon die.

> "There are so many things I should have done," he thought, and suddenly it was borne in upon him that life could have been sweet if only he had known thirty years ago what the results of the doctors' analysis would be at this far-distant point of the future that had rolled slowly but maliciously towards him and become the inescapable, arduous, and insupportable present. "If I had lived my life in the consciousness of the death, everything would have been different."[6]

6. Louis De Bernieres, *Corelli's Mandolin: A Novel* (New York: Vintage International, 1994) 27.

Cancer grabs us by the shirt collar and demands our attention. In an instant, we are no longer allowed to believe the seductive whisper that tells us we always have tomorrow. If we are lucky to live with cancer long enough, we understand that we had no right to demand a tomorrow in the first place.

I was a freshman in college when my paternal grandmother was very ill and in a Portland hospital. Greg's family lived in Portland, and he and I went to stay with his family so I could visit her. I spent hours at the hospital. The first time I held her hands I was shocked to see I held my hand. I realized we shared the same bone structure. We were alike and connected in this fundamental way. Her once beautiful face was now pale and spotted, with sunken cheeks. She slept mostly, giving me plenty of time to think.

I'm not sure how she felt about having grandchildren. One time when I was probably four, and Steve was six, she and my grandfather agreed to take care of us while my parents went out. Their mothball-smelling guestroom had two single beds. There was a gray file cabinet by the door. Grandma said goodnight and was gone, and Steve and I settled into bed.

"Hey, Julie?"

"Yeah."

"You see that file cabinet?"

"Yeah."

"There're monsters in that file cabinet. Goodnight."

I exploded with fear. I screamed. I grew hysterical. Floods of tears crashed down my face, while Steve complained about how he was trying to get some sleep. His snotty grumbling pissed me off, even then. But I was young enough to believe in monsters, and young enough to believe my brother. My grandparents kept trying to get me to stop crying, but they didn't think to ask me why I was crying. Finally, out of options, they called my parents to come pick us up.

With one question and a few open file drawers, I immediately calmed down.

My grandparents never babysat us again.

I did not know her well; even so, I don't remember ever hearing her laugh. In the hospital, I held her hand and saw in her wasted, frail body and bloodshot eyes that she was worn out with the work of living. I took a deep breath and thought that when it was my turn, I didn't want to have any regrets. When I am old and lying in the hospital bed, I want to close my eyes knowing that I tried to spend my life well. I knew that we all give our lives away to something. I didn't want to be in a bed with the wish that I could've lived my life differently.

Greg and I met Sonya soon after we moved to Oregon. Sonya was a feisty, petite German woman who, over the years of grooming our Cocker Spaniel, became a good friend. She was passionate about most things. She was passionate about her dogs, passionate about the rain in Oregon that never stopped. Sonya, bless her heart, often kept me in her garage-turned-grooming-spot to tell me about the latest thing that had caught her attention; or she would remember something about my life and ask for the latest details, offering all kinds of advice. When I told her we might move to the Midwest, she gasped.

"Oh, Julie, no! No! You don't want to move there. The weather! It's awful. Why would anyone want to live there? The snow, the cold. Horrible!" If I could hand pick my own German grandmother, I would pick Sonya in a heartbeat.

Sonya was also passionate about her husband. He had been diagnosed with kidney cancer some months before I discovered my tumor, and his decline was precipitous. He died within months. Sonya grieved for him with the same passion with which she had loved him. For months, when I came, she would burst into tears and tell me the story of his cancer, as if for the first time. "He went so fast, Julie. Oh, it was horrible. Horrible."

When Sonya heard about my diagnosis, she became very emotional. Some months later, when I came with my dog, she said, "How awful, Julie, how awful. Oh, Julie, when I heard the news, I couldn't believe it. Oh, I couldn't believe it. I said, 'poor Julie, poor Julie!' I couldn't believe it. How are you feeling? You look good. Oh, when I heard, I said, 'No! She is so young, she is so full of life. I can't believe it!' But you know, my sweet husband, he went so fast. I thought maybe he just had a stomachache. Maybe he ate something bad, or something that didn't agree with him. How could we know? But we found out he had cancer and then he was gone. But you, you are alive. He didn't have a chance. But you are alive. Where there's life, there's hope."

When she said that, I had two reactions. First, I wanted to explain to her just how serious my tumor was. I wanted to tell her that even though I looked normal, I had not yet escaped death. At that point, I'd made a few inroads into killing the cancer, only putting death off for a few months. This killing was excruciatingly slow, and the battle was not over, not over in the least.

The other thing I felt was shame. I stood in her tidy garage and felt tremendously humbled. That morning when I drove to Sonya's, I'd been feeling majorly sorry for myself. I was reveling in self-pity. My private little poor-me party was complete with black balloons and mournful dirges. But she was right. I was not dead. I was standing with her, and her husband was not. Sonya brought me back. Where there's life, there's hope.

7

✑

"No!"

Do not go gentle into that good night,
Rage, rage against the dying of the light.[1]

—Dylan Thomas

A MAN stands at the top of the mountain punching his fists angrily at a disinterested sky. His name is Job. His suffering and resultant anger are the result of a wager between God and Satan—literally "adversary." It all began one day when God was touting the faithfulness of his beloved Job, and Satan called him on it.

In the beginning, Job is a wealthy, healthy, upright man. So much so, God boasts that Job is one of God's favorites, declaring him a perfect example of faithfulness. God's adversary, Satan, challenges God. "Does Job fear God for naught? Hast thou not put a hedge about him and his house and all that he has on every side? Thou has blest the work of his hands, and his possessions have increased in

---

1. Dylan Thomas, in William Sloane Coffin, *Living the Truth in a World of Illusions* (San Francisco: Harper & Row, 1985) 56.

the land" (Job 1:9–10). In other words, "Big deal. Job's got it good, why wouldn't he be faithful to you? That's not faithfulness. That's knowing what side his pita's buttered on. Take away all of the sweet benefits you give him, then see just how upright your Job is."

To prove a point, God allows Satan to devastate Job's life. Job loses his wealth, his home, his family, and finally his health. He is reduced to a penniless man covered in sores.

The book of Job is not a theodicy, written to defend the ways of God to a suffering humanity, nor is it written to hold up a man of patience. It is a story about what it means to be a person of faith. In holding up Job as an example of integrity, the book flies in the face of the conventional wisdom of the day. The "Wisdom Tradition" was one way to understand the ways of God in Job's day; it explained suffering as punitive. If you are suffering, it is your own fault. You are suffering because you did something wrong. God is trying to teach you a lesson, or maybe God is simply punishing you for what you've done. Either way, the reason you are in pain lies in your past or in your heart. Come clean, confess, and your suffering will end.

Job's friend Eliphaz says, "Think now, who that was innocent ever perished? Or where were the upright cut off? As I have seen, those who plow iniquity and sow trouble reap the same. By the breath of God they perish, and by the blast of his anger they are consumed" (Job 4:7–9). He is only trying to remind Job what they both know to be true: God is just and blesses the innocent; only the guilty suffer.

Later, another friend, Bildad, is more blunt. "Does God pervert justice? Or does the Almighty pervert the right? If your children have sinned against him, he has delivered them into the power of their transgression" (Job 8:3–4). To Bildad the world makes sense. If you do what is right, God will bless you. Perhaps an ancestor of Bernie Seigel, Bildad details for Job the reasons he suffers. If Job would only confess, his suffering would end.

But Job refuses to confess what is not true; he insists throughout the book that he has done nothing wrong.

> Today my complaint is rebellious. My hand is heavy in
> spite of my praying. Oh that I knew where I might find
> God, that I might come before God's seat! I would lay my
> case before God, and fill my mouth with arguments . . .
>   I will take God to court and present my case. I will
> show that it is not I who have brought this upon myself.
> (Job 23:1–3)

Job's argument is with God. Job ignores his wife's amazingly helpful advice to curse God and die. He refuses to give in to the advice of his friends and confess. He never wavers from declaring his innocence. He chooses to take God seriously by bringing his challenge to God.

As one interpreter, Gerald Janzen, writes: "Job will not sue for peace under the present circumstances. In Jeremiah's terms, that would be to say 'Peace, peace' when there is no peace. Somehow a peace on those terms would be a betrayal of the divine-human relationship. By a strange paradox, the only loyal act under the circumstances is rebellion."[2]

In the midst of his suffering, Job maintains his integrity by refusing to take responsibility for his suffering, and instead calls God to account. Nicholas Wolterstorff, in his journal on the death of his son, writes, "Suffering is the shout of 'No' by one's whole existence to that over which one suffers—the shout of 'No' by nerves and gut and gland and heart to pain, to death . . . to injustice."[3] Job's faith, Job's *integrity*, is the shout of "No" to the unjust suffering in his life, a "No!" he shouts to God. This is, in part, what faith is. Taking God on. Shouting "No!"

Both Job, who refused the current wisdom of the day, and Jacob, who wrestled with all he had against the angel, discovered the power to say no: no to circumstances that were bent on defining them.

2. J. Gerald Janzen, *Job*, Interpretation (Atlanta: John Knox, 1985) 165.

3. Nicholas Wolterstorff, *Lament for a Son* (Grand Rapids: Eerdmans, 1987) 96.

I made a decision early on to go through my experience honestly. For me to shout "No" meant to resist many of the ways the label "cancer patient" tried to define me. Throughout the ravages of the storm, I developed my own survival tactics: ways I could resist its attempt to take over and destroy my life, not only physically, but psychically. The tactics were simple—a few rules, some basic assumptions. Still, they had terrific power to help me, and my family and friends, get through.

Shouting "No!" has real power. Not only emotionally, but sometimes physically. Speaking of people who had gotten well against all odds, Marc Ian Barasch explains,

> [These people] did everything from chemo to carrot juice. What they had in common was that they'd all decided to look upon their disease as unique, just as they were unique, and then find a path to healing that drew upon their own enthusiasm, beliefs, and coping mechanisms . . . If you treat illness as a personal journey, you're more likely to marshal your own maximum resources both inner and outer, in addition to finding an appropriate treatment regimen.
>
> The people who healed tended to work at getting well on all fronts. They found social support, faith, and purpose, encountered deep emotions, did things they loved and usually chose a more healthy lifestyle, including dietary changes—though not always; one just ate greasy hamburgers.[4]

My primary rule was that I would never be at the hospital alone. We coordinated schedules each month, so that someone was with me most of the time.

The second was more of an understanding than a rule. Even though I was bald, hooked up to an IV, in pj's or hospital gowns, I was still Julie. I still had a sense of humor; I still loved good beer; I enjoyed music. Dad bought me a portable CD player, and I lis-

4. Mark Ian Barasch in Derrick Jensen, "Body Language: A Conversation with Mark Ian Barasch on Illness and Healing," *The Sun* January 2000, 5–6.

tened to Van Morrison and Bonnie Raitt. I refused to eat bad food. At that time OHSU had a definite food problem. One night my brother-in-law Doug tried to feed me the hospital's pathetic excuse for spaghetti. It was a dreary clump of fat soggy noodles, covered with what had been, in its previous life, red sauce. Doug brought the fork to my mouth as if I was one of his young daughters. He was slow in doing it, giving me plenty of time to see up close just exactly what my dinner was. I ate a few bites to humor him, but that was it. I had a brain tumor, but there was nothing wrong with my taste buds. I may have been bald and in a hospital bed without many culinary options, but I still had standards. I was still Julie.

If you let it, illness has the power to sum you up with a medical diagnosis: Cancer Patient, Leukemia Patient, Heart Patient. Hospitals do much to encourage this medical reductionism. In the hospital you lose all privacy—anyone can enter your room at any time. It's worse in a teaching hospital. There, I was not only "Julie, Cancer Patient," but, "Julie, interactive scientific-teaching tool." Neurologists, anesthesiologists, you name it; they all have their groupies. To his credit, Dr. Neuwelt does not allow the disruption program to be a teaching program; his patients are spared some group intrusions.

Still, on a regular basis, clumps of interns in white coats with stethoscopes swarmed into my room. They held clipboards and stood at the end of my bed. They tried to peer over one another's shoulders to get a glimpse at my chart, then jot down a few notes while grunting knowingly to themselves. There was no eye contact or any meaningful conversation. Certainly no touching or the polite question, how are you feeling? They turned away and left together as if on cue, like migrating birds, off to their next medical exhibit.

But there are unintentional ways of reductionism too. One day Steve was rolling me back to my room in a wheelchair and describing how his life was changed because I had a brain tumor.

"How is it different?" I asked him.

"I have a sister who is a cancer patient," he explained, as if his life was made up of a variety of declarations, and now this one needed to find a home in his consciousness with the others. But throughout my journey, I was always more comfortable with the word *tumor* than the word *cancer*. *Tumor* was specific. You could point to it on a scan. It was a visible spot to destroy. But cancer? The word *cancer* exploded into a scary world. It was vague, vast, threatening, and out of control.

But someone out in the existential world seemed to be paying attention, and that someone wanted to twist the cancer knife into my consciousness, because as Steve spoke and we were coming off the elevator, the wall opposite informed us we were on the floor for Adult Oncology.

Yes, I am a cancer patient. But I'm still Julie. I may be a temporary resident on the Adult oncology floor, but this is temporary! Do you hear me? Temporary! And I am still Julie. Still Julie. I tried to live this out the best I could.

My rebellion started every month as soon as I stepped into the hospital. The first day of my admission I spent running around the campus having various tests—blood test, hearing test, CT scan. I was admitted, but that didn't mean that I needed to lie in bed all day. Sometime in the middle of the year, I had been admitted. Steve and I were sitting around waiting for my next test, so we decided to play Nerts in the hallway. In Nerts, both players play off the central card piles in an attempt to empty their hand first. It requires fast reactions and great hand-eye coordination, and Steve cut me no slack. There we were, sitting on the floor, slamming cards down, other cards flying, when Annie came up. "OK, Julie, time for your neurological exam. Close your eyes, reach out your hand and touch your finger to your nose."

One monthly test was a CAT scan. The schedule was on-call. Translation: sit around your hospital room and wait for a call from CT. The nurses try and help out by giving you a rough estimate of when CT will call. On my fourth admit, I sat around most of the afternoon, expecting a call any moment. Finally, my parents arrived with dinner—Italian. They came in the room, and with them rode a whiff of garlic and Parmesan. The noodles were cooked to perfection, dripping a nice white-wine and butter sauce. As I brought my second forkful to my mouth, there was a knock on my door. I opened it to see a teenager in a green transport shirt behind a wheelchair.

"I'm here to take you to CT. "

"I'm not going." I wiped my mouth with my napkin. "I've been waiting all afternoon. My parents just arrived with dinner, and I'm going to stay and eat it."

He took a step back, as shocked as a suitor at the front door being rejected for a date. "Can you *do* that?"

"I just did."

"Hang on, I'm going to check this out with one of the nurses."

An hour later, there was another knock on the door. I opened it to see a behemoth of a man in a green shirt with a wheelchair.

"Time for your scan," he grunted in a gravelly voice that said, "Don't mess with me." In case I didn't get the message, he added, "they send me for the tough ones." He rocked a little on his feet and stared at me with a hint of challenge. As if little, weak, barely 120 pounds of me would be any kind of match for the Sylvester Stallone of Transports.

Although we never talked about it, Steve had his own ways of rebelling. One of them was to make labels for my hospital gown the mornings I went into surgery. They said things like, "Handle with TLC"; "If found, please return to Greg Love, (503) . . ."; "Hand-wash only, dry flat, no bleach"; "Made in the USA." The surgeons and techs got used to looking for them as I was being rolled into the operating room: "What does it say this time?"

A hospital diet was not mandatory for me, so Steve scoped out a few take-out places with really good food and spoiled me with gourmet pizza, Japanese Bento boxes, locally brewed beer.

Forrest Gump was new in theaters during the fifth month of treatment. My tests were all done. When my tests were all done, we were simply going to sit around to wait for the morning. Then Steve got the idea of going out for pizza and catching *Forrest Gump*. In previous disruptions, I'd often gone down to the cafeteria for dinner—there was no reason for me to stay on the floor.

That night I saw my nurse in the hall.

"I'm going to get dinner," I told her.

"OK, great. Down in the cafeteria?"

"Hey, maybe so, that's a good idea!" I smiled.

Lowering her voice and glancing around conspiratorially, she said, "Just be back by ten."

Steve and I drove to Pizzacato, a gourmet pizza place on Portland's hip Northwest Twenty-Third Avenue. The street was lit up with white twinkly lights; music pumped out of various restaurants and bars. The street was pulsing with all manner of humanity. Twenty-year-old women in high heels and short skirts walked the sidewalk with men dressed in trendy black jackets. Women walking arm in arm, dressed in tight jeans and sleeveless tops, peeked into store windows; an African American man sitting on the corner sidewalk played guitar and sang to the stars. There was a wait at Pizzacato, which was entirely fine with me. I loved being out of the hospital. I loved that I wasn't sitting in my room with nothing to do but contemplate the morning. And I especially loved the fact that my brother was spending time with me in this sneaky, disobedient way. We sat on the high stools that circled small round tables, listening to jazz. We ordered a Margherita pizza. The crust was thin with a nice crunch and subtle layer of cheese. The garlic was perfect—not too strong, but strong enough to light up the fresh basil and warm tomatoes. The Hefeweizen washed it down with just the right combination of yeast and hops. It was the first time pizza had tasted like freedom.

When we went to see *Forrest Gump*, I hid my hospital bracelet under my sleeve, just in case some nosey teenage usher happened to glance my way, see with his excellent night vision that I was a medical escapee, and actually care enough to turn me in. There were quite a few people sitting around, especially for a midweek showing. I sat close enough to Steve to feel the warmth of his arm next to mine.

My rule-obeying voice piped up, rather unconvincingly. *Julie! You really shouldn't do this, you know. You should be back in the hospital, safe and sound. I'm pretty sure this is against the rules.* But the stronger, beer-emboldened voice stomped all over that. *Frankly, I don't give a rat's ass! I am loving this. I am totally loving this!! So just shut up, sit back and enjoy the show.* Steve and I laughed and cried, more than willing to get lost in someone else's story. We snuck back into the hospital, guilty kids who'd stayed out way past curfew.

The next morning before surgery when we were trying to figure out what I should put on my gown, Jody said, "Hey! Tape your ticket stub to your gown."

On the gurney on my way to OR, Annie looked at my gown.

"Man, Julie, you got me in so much trouble this morning," she said, keeping pace with the gurney.

Timing is everything. That morning the disruption-program staff had a meeting to discuss patients leaving the hospital after they'd been admitted. Seems I wasn't the first to think of it. Admitted patients walking around town was a huge liability for the hospital.

So, rolling down the hall on the way to surgery, Annie and a few others were talking about how the hospital was now insisting the staff work to keep the patients in the hospital. We mostly laughed about it, with Annie trying her hardest to be serious. When I entered the operating room, the doctors and techs checked out my gown. When they saw my ticket stub, they said, "You went to see *Forrest Gump*?" trying to sound punishing and serious.

But then one of them said, "Hey, I heard that's a pretty good movie. What d'ya think?"

"It's not bad."

We talked about the movie as I crawled onto the operating table. Even there, in a room crammed with huge beeping machines and people hidden behind masks and scrubs—a most inhuman place—even there we had a moment of utter normalcy.

Shouting No! takes many forms. A movie review can be a shout of resistance, as it was in that sterile place.

Dan, a good friend of Greg's, often stopped by to visit, and one time before my seventh disruption, Dan brought some outstanding

Chinese food: chicken with cashew nuts, and a beer for each of us. M. J., my nurse, sweet M. J., just about had a seizure.

"My God! You can't have beer on the floor! What in the world are you thinking?!"

Two months later, when Dan came by again, he poured the beer into big, plastic, sober cups.

When Job took God to court, he refused to accept the day's wisdom by declaring he was somehow at fault for his misery. Instead, he stood on the mountain, searching the skies. "Where are you? Where are you? Come out and answer me." It was to God that he directed his fists. He punched the indifferent sky.

His protest echoed many protests found in the Psalms.

> God, my God,
> why have you abandoned me—
> far from my cry, my words of pain?
> I call by day, you do not answer;
> I call by night, but find no rest.
>
> You are the Holy One enthroned,
> the Praise of Israel.
> Our people trusted, they trusted you;
> you rescued them.
> To you they cried, and they were saved;
> they trusted and were not shamed.
>
> But I am a worm, hardly human,
> despised by all, mocked by the crowd.
> All who see me jeer at me,
> sneer at me, shaking their heads:
> "You relied on God; let God help you!
> If God loves you, let God save you!"[5]
>
> Psalm 22:1–9

---

5. International Commission on English in the Liturgy, *The Psalter* (Chicago: Liturgy Training, 1994) Psalm 22.

In *The Message of the Psalms,* Walter Brueggemann describes three different categories of psalms: orientation, disorientation, and reorientation. Psalm 22 belongs to the category of Disorientation. These psalms declare that the world no longer makes sense. The psalmist's world is utterly devastated, and the broken psalmist brings a complaint to God. I am a worm. I am poured out like water. All who see me mock me. "Psalms of disorientation express the incoherence that we experience in the world," Brueggemann writes. These psalms tell it like it is.

> It is no wonder that the church has intuitively avoided these psalms . . . They lead us into the presence of God where everything is not polite and civil. They cause us to think unthinkable thoughts and utter unutterable words. Perhaps worse, they lead us away from the comfortable religious claims of "modernity" in which everything is managed and controlled. In our modern experience, it is believed that enough power and knowledge can tame the terror and eliminate the darkness. Use of the psalms of darkness may be judged by the world to be acts of unfaith and failure, but for the trusting community, their use is an act of bold faith because it insists that the world must be experienced as it really is and not in some pretended way.[6]

Just as the opposite of love is not hate but indifference, the opposite of faith is not doubt but apathy. To fight an adversary, one needs an adversary to fight. To suffer honestly I could only say what was true. All that I knew was that I was fighting for my life. Where in this hell were you, you who claim to be the God of life?

Breuggemann again:

> [Using psalms of disorientation] is a bold act because it insists that all such experiences of disorder are a proper subject of discourse with God. To withhold parts of life

6. Walter Brueggemann, *The Message of the Psalms: A Theological Commentary,* Augsburg Old Testament Studies (Minneapolis: Augsburg, 1984) 53.

> from that conversation is in fact to withhold part of life
> from the sovereignty of God. Thus these psalms make
> the important connection: everything must be brought
> to speech, and everything brought to speech must be ad-
> dressed to God, who is the final reference for all of life.[7]

It was really hard for me to verbally, consciously pray during
these times. I rarely spoke literal words; my "prayers" were more
thoughts and images and feelings. If I could put them to words,
they would've sounded something like this:

> Dear God, it's me. I'm having a tough time right now. And
> to be frank, there are moments these days when I wonder
> where you are. I've staked my life on the conviction that
> you are utterly a God of life, entirely a God of love. And
> yet, here I am fighting for this life you've given me and I
> do not know where you are. *I do not know where you are.*
> And the promises made at my baptism, those that said I
> am your child, they are but a distant echo, fading further
> away as the news continues to be bad. And I hear only
> silence in this place where no one laughs.

Hymns, on the other hand, came to me and I sang them to
myself most days.

> Be Thou my vision, O Lord of my heart;
> Nought be all else to me save that Thou art—
> Thou my best thought, by day or by night,
> Waking or sleeping, Thy presence my light.
>
> Riches I heed not, nor vain empty praise,
> Thou mine inheritance, now and always:
> Thou and Thou only, first in my heart,
> Great God of heaven, my treasure Thou art.

This Irish hymn, with a text from the eighth century, was my
favorite. Van Morrison sang it on his CD *Hymns to the Silence*,
and listening to it while I lay in the hospital bed, I remembered

7. Ibid., 52.

so many times in the past when I had sung those words with my whole heart.

> Be Thou my wisdom, and Thou my true word;
> I even with Thee and Thou with me, Lord;
> Heart of my own heart, whatever befall,
> Still be my vision, O Ruler of all.[8]

It is often said, when one sings they pray twice.

---

8. "Be Thou My Vision," in *The Presbyterian Hymnal* (Louisville: Westminster John Knox, 1990) #339.

8

⚮

Summary

It was the best of summers; it was the worst of summers.
—a la Charles Dickens

THE BEGINNING of the summer was hopeful; the news about my tumor was good. By June, I'd had twelve disruptions over six months. I was at the halfway point. The tumor began to shrink. Dr. Neuwelt's seriousness took on a positive spin. Still unwilling to make any promises, he was clearly pleased with the response we were getting. We had every reason to be optimistic and expect the tumor to continue to shrink.

But this news came with a price.

By the summer, I also began to notice a significant decline in my hearing. When Greg spoke to me from across the room, I couldn't understand. When he spoke with his back to me, I needed to ask, "come again?" A few months before, I'd met a woman in the program who was also fighting a pinealblastoma. She was close to my age and further down the treatment-hell road than I was. Once, we were sitting together in our wheelchairs in the hallway, waiting for our CT scans.

"How many treatments have you had?" I asked her.

"What?"

Speaking a bit louder, "what number is this treatment for you?"

"Oh. Um. I think it's the eighth one."

"Wow. You're getting there."

"I'm sorry, what'd you say?"

"I said I'm impressed. You're two-thirds of the way through. That's great! It's a drag that we might lose some hearing."

"You know, I realized that I was losing my hearing, so I went to a healing service and I got it back!" She was clearly happy about this.

I nodded and smiled. "Great! I'm happy for you."

Meanwhile, I was mildly irritated at how much work it was to talk to her, and realized this might be what other people would experience with me.

Greg and I made an appointment to speak with Dr. Neuwelt.

Dr. Neuwelt was extremely reluctant to make a change in the chemo drugs. I assumed it was a simple matter of using a different drug that would be equally effective, and stressed to him the extent of damage to my hearing. He was marginally concerned. It wasn't until I asked enough questions that I understood the drug, carboplatin, which was destroying my hearing, was the one drug most effective in killing my tumor. While he ordered monthly hearing tests to monitor hearing changes, and while there were other patients he'd taken off carboplatin, he wanted to push me to the limit. My tumor was responding dramatically. Dr. Neuwelt was not a betting man, but this tumor upped the ante—there were very few success stories with pinealblastomas. Neuwelt put all his chips on this hearing-killing drug. There might be a chance we could beat the tumor if we kept using it.

So. There it was, my future in a nutshell: Deaf or dead? Hmmmm. Call me crazy, but I'll go with deaf.

On the western edge of the Olympic Peninsula in Washington, a hiking trail runs along the coast. It is sliver of the larger Olympic National Forest that takes up most of the peninsula. Greg and I hiked this trail the summer after we married. The trail runs along the beach, crossing over cliffs and beachheads. We started on one beach, and then hiked up and over a hillside to the next beach. Every beach was unique—some sandy, others covered in boulders. Some buried under piles of logs.

It was a wonderful, sunny day. We saw all kinds of wildlife. A baby harbor seal was curled up alone on one beach, waiting for his mama; a bald eagle coasted in large, lazy circles over our heads. In one forest we shared the trail with a few deer. I was having a great time with my new husband; this marriage thing was all right.

But then we walked the length of one beautiful sandy beach only to meet a steep cliff. The cliff must have been forty feet high. The only way up was a rope ladder, and it hung there, flopping back and forth in the breeze as if to say, "you can use me if you want, but I ain't makin' no promises—you're on your own."

Greg started up without hesitation. As he climbed, I stood on the beach watching him. "Get back down here. It's time to turn around." He continued to climb.

"I'm not climbing that." I yelled. "No way. No how. Time to turn around and head back."

But he kept on. "Come on, Julie. It's no big deal. Really, it's fine."

He was so calm, taking it all in stride. I thought, maybe he's right. I started to climb and got about half-way up before it hit me full force. *Wait just a minute!! What are you doing, dangling from a cliff by this thin, unreliable rope!! Don't look down, my God! DON'T LOOK DOWN! Don't look up! Don't move! The next step could be your last! DO NOT MOVE!* I was frozen with fear.

Greg wasn't fazed. "Oh, come on, Julie. You can do it. It's no big deal. You're almost there."

His voice struck the perfect tone. It wasn't belittling, shaming me up the hill. Nor did he sound at all worried. He was simply waiting for me at the top. I figured he must be right; it wasn't that big of a deal. If he believed I could do it, I probably could. I climbed the rest of the way. It wasn't until we got back to our hotel room that night that he told me he was a little freaked out about the ladder, but he guessed that if he showed any fear, there would be no way I would climb it.

After I survived my first several disruptions, I couldn't imagine going on a backpack trip. But Greg could. Catherine and Mark thought it was a great idea too, and the four of us took a five-day trip to the Olympic National Forest.

Before the trip, Greg insisted I get a hearing aid.

Frankly, I didn't want to get a hearing aid. I knew this wasn't rational, but who has ever accused me of being rational? Wearing a hearing aid signified that I was beginning the long departure from the hearing world, and I wasn't ready to leave it, not yet. If I was really honest, I was terribly afraid that a hearing aid would not help. What then? What would I do? If I'm the embodiment of irrationality, Greg is my counterpart. He wanted me to get a hearing aid, hoping that it would help me hear the birds on our trip.

Because I loved that he wanted me to hear the birds, I went to OHSU's audiologist. I brought a friend, just in case. Just in case the hearing aid failed and I found out the world would inexorably fade away from me as I fought this damn brain tumor. I needed someone to hold me, just in case.

The audiologist put something in my ear, and I heard a beep. It was an electronic beep, like the sound of an oven timer. And then he spoke; his voice sounded like the recording of an answering machine, flattened and sharpened by its passage through the hearing aid. I sighed. The sound was not perfect by any means. But it was a sound. I couldn't afford to be picky.

The Olympic National Forest is a vast, protected area with mountains at its center. A highway runs the perimeter of the park, and no other roads pass through it. And because it is a rainforest, practically every inch—branch, tree, rock—is covered in some manifestation of green. Moss, ferns, saplings—all fight it out for a place to grow. Moss droops down from tree limbs like ancient spider webs in a long abandoned house.

We hiked along the river valley, gaining little elevation. Thankfully the rainforest did not live up to its name, and the weather stayed sunny the entire trip. Because Mark and I love chocolate, he brought five pounds of it, one for each day!

Given that my immune system was basically shot, we used Catherine and Mark's new water purifier, then boiled my water for ten minutes. A few days we didn't boil it until morning—nothing like a little tea water for the trail! I was a full member of the group. I carried my pack, helped set up the tent. I walked the same number of miles. I was bald, but no one cared. We talked about the tumor a little, but we talked about all kinds of things. I love them all for that trip.

As I mentioned earlier, we then spent another week at the Oregon coastal town, my second home, with our good friends Hunter and Susan.

I convinced Dr. Neuwelt to delay my July treatment for a week. "Guess everyone needs a vacation," he reluctantly mumbled.

Before I became sick, I'd been visiting a woman in the church who was fighting cancer. I visited her in her darkened living room.

There the shades were drawn, and her voice was frail. But when she heard about my diagnoses and the fact that by the summer I was working part-time and taking some adventures, she began taking trips to the beach, and spending time with her grandchildren. "If Julie can do it, then so can I," she told her worried daughters.

When my friends treated me like Julie, albeit Julie fighting an important battle, I was strengthened for the battle. "You can do it, Julie. It's no big deal . . ." I discovered they were right. They sent me this message in all kinds of ways: on the backpack trip: walking miles on the coast, riding bikes in Vancouver, BC, laughing with me. When people in your life believe in you, there's also the message that your survival matters to them, that life would not be the same if you were not there to share it.

Greg was a master at making me feel whole, healthy, and a necessary part of his life. He cared for me, but he didn't belittle me. Just as he had set up the backpack trip and had insisted on my first hearing aid, he spent a lot of time thinking of creative ways to make my days more enjoyable.

One day that summer, our friend Dan called to invite Greg and me to dinner. Unfortunately, on the day he suggested, we had plans to go to Catherine and Mark's for dinner. For some reason, Dan insisted on having us come that day; because Dan and his wife, Julie, didn't live far from Catherine and Mark in Portland, we decided to stop by early in the evening for a glass of wine.

It is amazing how stubborn a mind can be—or maybe it's just my mind? When we walked into Dan's kitchen, there were all these people standing around in a half-circle, and they all yelled, "surprise!" I was confused. Mom and Dad were there. Steve and Jody were with them. Steve Wilhelm was standing next to them with a wineglass in his hand. My uncle and aunt and cousins were there. So many of them were from Seattle. My first thought was, "Damn! They came all this way and we can't stay, we're already late for Catherine and Mark's!" until I spotted Catherine and Mark. It was then that I let out a little yelp and burst into tears.

Greg had organized the party to celebrate that I was halfway through the program. We partied and laughed and ate delicious hors-d'oeuvres, something Greg had insisted on.

I felt tremendously lucky to have Greg and so many wonderful, faithful friends.

That summer was also the worst of summers. Not everyone in my life chose to travel with me. There were others that I thought loved me, but who left me to fend for myself.

The church was moving closer to calling a new pastor, which meant that they needed to decide on the details of the position: salary, vacation, and the like. The interim pastor, A. C., convinced the congregation that they needed a terrific salary to draw talent. To do that, he argued, they had to close my position. While I knew the church was planning to become a one-pastor church, I also knew that I wasn't costing them a lot, and assumed that they loved me and would see me through my treatments. My health insurance, which wasn't great when it came to deductibles, was amazingly generous when it came to disability coverage. I was able to work up to half-time and still be considered fully disabled. My insurance paid sixty percent of my salary and covered my pension and benefits. This left the church with the responsibility of only forty percent of my cash salary. I was a steal.

In the Presbyterian system, certain decisions are made by the church's elected ruling body, or Session, others by the entire congregation. The decision to call or let go pastors is voted on by the congregation.

The Sunday of the meeting, Greg refused to go to church.

I preached the morning of the vote. On any normal Sunday, when I preach, two voices rattle around in my head. The first is the sermon itself. As I speak, I worry. *I hope to God it makes sense and I'm not wasting everyone's time with senseless, narcissistic babble.* And then there is the second voice. *How to catch the attention of*

Mr. Sanderson in the back who's looking out the window? Make sure you stress this point, and slow down with the story. This is a critical moment in the sermon. Are people watching? Are they paying attention? Do you have them? Is that young mom with you or is she daydreaming? Look them in the eye, Julie. Make sure they know you're talking to them, each one.

From my perspective, the sermon that day couldn't have carried any more gravity. I spoke of listening for God's guidance. I looked everyone in the eye. I preached my heart out. I wanted them to know just what they would be missing. A part of me could not believe that these people would vote to let me go, downsize me, set me adrift, close the door on my livelihood, when there was the sticky little question of my brain tumor. My survival was still very much in question, a situation all the more complicated because Greg was still working on his dissertation; that is, he was unemployed.

They loved me. I was convinced of it. They had told me so uncountable times over the years. We'd had lively women's retreats, young-adult Bible studies, family camps in the summer. Kids ran in and out from behind grownup legs in the coffee hour, wiggled in worship, decorated the church with their Sunday school art. The congregation was made of all kinds of people. It was alive and thriving. Surely they could find it in their hearts, and budget, to continue to travel the way with me.

The morning of the vote, over twenty children came up for the children's talk. When I sat with them, my sweet little loved ones, they looked up at me with such innocent, trusting eyes. They had no idea that I might be leaving them. I had to bite my lip to keep from crying.

It is not politically correct for the pastor whose position is the topic of the congregational meeting to be present while the congregation deliberates. Screw that, I thought. If they are going to do this to me, they are going to do this in my presence.

I sat down in one of the pews near the front.

"I am calling this meeting to order," A. C. said to a quiet congregation.

"There is a motion before you to close the current Associate Pastor position."

Here it comes, I thought. Someone is going to stand up and say how utterly wrong this motion is. Someone, someone will have the courage to speak the truth and explain the fact that A. C. was the driving force behind this motion. Someone will say they have treasured the years I spent with them, and that the church was a different place because of me. I looked around at those faces. *Who would it be? David, would you speak, Greg and I spent endless hours sitting with you and Johanna, drinking coffee at your kitchen table, talking late into the night. You even invited us to be present at the home birth of Morgan. Would you say how wrong this all is? How about Cindi? Remember how I stayed the night with you when your drug addict of an ex-husband was shot by the cops in Portland? Remember how I baptized Elsa, and then years later married you to that wonderful man of yours? Would you stand up and say something? Or Carol. If you stood up tall and spoke loudly, most people would hear you. How many family celebrations did I share with you and all of your adult children? How many afternoons did I spend sipping your tea and talking for hours with you and Platt? I remember you once told me I was the only pastor Platt ever had time for. Remember how he made a notebook filled with copies of all of my sermons? Wouldn't you say something?*

By the time my attention returned to the deliberations, I realized they were discussing my severance package.

It was happening. They were closing my position. No one was going to stop it.

"What about covering Julie's health benefits?" David asked.

"Do you think she needs it? There've been times when I've been without health benefits." A. C. was perfectly serious.

My body started shaking and I shot him a look. Were you fighting a malignant brain tumor at the time? I wanted to ask. I glared at him and thought there must be a special place in hell for people like him.

Then he called for the vote to close the Associate position.

"All those in favor?" A majority of grim ayes rang through the church.

"All those opposed?" A few weak nays haunted the air in reply.

"The ayes have it!" A. C. declared.

I was no longer their pastor.

I tried to run for the backdoor. People were coming up to me, "Julie, I just want to say . . ." I pushed them aside, dodged their faces. I had to get away. Away from these people who were trying to talk to me, trying to explain themselves, trying to make themselves feel better. I ran upstairs to my office and slammed the door, half expecting that someone would come find me. I sobbed and threw things and paced and sobbed some more. Finally, I blew my nose and sat on the couch. I waited until I couldn't hear any voices, and then waited some more. When I finally came back downstairs, the building was empty. The sanctuary looked as it always looked, its empty pews waiting for the next time people would gather and call on God to join them. Waiting for the next time the people would sing songs and pray and laugh. Waiting for the next time the organist would play the newly renovated organ, and the children would come forward for the children's sermon during the service. The sanctuary bore no signs of my broken heart.

The next day Angie stopped by. Angie was a longtime member of the church. Her wisdom was hard won; life had wounded her deeply with the loss of a son to AIDS, and the continual struggle of caring for an adult daughter suffering from a mental illness. She was holding a small box of See's candy.

"I guess we're schmucks, aren't we?"

"You know, I think its OK. There was no way I could work with A. C. anyway." I told her.

Believe it or not, at that moment, that was how I felt. But I knew not what I was saying. It could've been that my attention was solely on the battle before me—there was nothing left in my heart that could deal with any more betrayals. Or it could've been that my heart was so utterly shattered that, like the physical shock of a deep wound, emotional shock had set in.

One thing was clear: I was set adrift. I no longer knew what I was doing in Albany; I no longer had a way to explain myself. With the congregation's decision, I lost a central way to think of myself. I was no longer the associate pastor at United Presbyterian Church. I lost my professional designation and my place in the community. The relationships I'd built over the years were gone. It made me question the time I'd spent with these people. I could not help but question their expressions of love and concern. If you love someone, you don't leave them jobless and without health care in the midst of a battle for survival.

Gerald Sittser is a professor of religion at Whitworth College in Spokane, Washington. In the fall of 1991 he was driving home from visiting an Indian reservation in eastern Washington with his wife, his mother, and his children. A drunk driver hit them head on, going eighty-five miles an hour. Sittser lost his wife, his mother, and his youngest daughter in that accident.

He reflects how his loss affected his sense of identity:

> Our sense of personal identity depends largely on the roles we play and the relationships we have. What we do and who we know contributes significantly to how we understand ourselves. Catastrophic loss is like undergoing an amputation of our identity. It is not like the literal amputation of a limb. Rather, it is more like the amputation of the self from the self. It is the amputation of the self as a professional, if one has lost a job. Or the self as a husband, if one has lost a spouse through divorce or death. Or the self as an energetic and productive person, if one has lost good health . . . It is the amputation of the self we once were or wanted to be, the self we can no longer be or become.[1]

1. Gerald Sittser, *A Grace Disguised: How the Soul Grows through Loss* (Grand Rapids: Zondervan, 1995) 70.

∞

For over eight years I could not talk about what happened without crying. Whenever I drove the section of I-5 that passed Albany, tears puddled in my eyes. The wound stayed open, refusing to heal. I'm here to tell you, some pithy sayings sound good, but don't believe them. Time does not heal all wounds. In fact, over time wounds can fester and become more painful.

I was only able to write about the event three years after the vote.

Journal entry, June 29, 1987

I ran into B. A. tonight. To be honest, I'd gotten lazy. I used to be so diligent—to check out her house before I got close and could be sighted. But, it's been literally years since I have seen her; since she orchestrated much of the changes that led to my position being closed at the church.

Jim [our pastoral counselor through it all] has said that of the two formative events of my adult life, the tumor and the church, his sense is that the pain of the church letting me go in the midst of my struggle for my life has been more traumatic for me than the tumor itself.

B. A. was surprised and clearly happy to see me, rushing over with her neighbor to say hello. Nowhere to turn, no longer any way to ignore and walk by, I stopped. Brief introductions were made, sidewalk chit chat. Then, "I've been meaning for so long to come see you. I keep telling myself, 'I've got to go up and see Julie'" She searched my face. Nothing. "We were close," she explained to her neighbor, with a nervous glance toward me. With no response, she added, "at least I thought we were."

When her neighbor wandered home, I was left with only her face. "I've been meaning to come say I'm sorry about all that." Laughing a bit, a big smile on her chubby face.

I looked in her eyes for a brief moment. "All that"? I thought. To what part are you referring? The part where you acted to call A. C.—a controlling, oversexed stuffed shirt—to come "save our church"? Or was it when you joined him to push the Session to close my position because, "there simply isn't money in the budget," and then watched the church raise $250,000 for a new elevator? Or, would all of that have been O.K., except for the sticky little detail that I was in the midst of treatment for a brain tumor?

You are a woman who put your priorities for the church before the welfare of someone you claim to have cared about.

How do I respond? "It's O.K. Don't worry about it"? Declare your sins forgiven and bless you on your way?

Forgiveness only happens with true repentance, and some awareness of the implications of what one has done. Somewhere the truth has to be told in order to get on with things.

The well of grief, the deep, deep well of sorrow, is one I carry. To say you care for, even dare to use the word "love" me—and then leave me in the midst of my life's battle, to take away the source and security of my livelihood, while it is that very life that is in question . . . How can that be forgiven on the sidewalk, with a smile and a few words? The water is cold and deep in the well of sorrow. And dark, so dark. A casual mention of a vague attempt to apologize is a mosquito on the water's surface. A small insult, a pesky irritant. Nothing more.

I glanced at her eyes for any hint of awareness, any acknowledgment of the absurdity of her words. There was nothing but gray.

A silent moment. A breath. Then, "I need to get going."

9

⚭

My God, My God...

THIS WILL not happen to you, I insisted over and over to myself,
a silent mantra. I clung to my coffee mug as if to a life ring, I
breathed deeply, trying to calm the rising panic in me. I was sitting in
Boccherini's, a coffee shop in Albany, talking with a woman who'd had
a brain tumor. Albany was a small enough community, under 40,000,
that anyone struck with a brain tumor had a certain notoriety. I'd
heard that her brain tumor was successfully treated with radiation.
My blood-brain barrier treatments had been wildly successful, but
there was one spot that refused to go away. Because my doctors were
discussing radiation treatment, I was looking into options. I wanted
to meet this woman to find out about her program.

She was about ten years older than me. Her brown hair framed
her pretty face—she looked a little like Mary Tyler Moore. She smiled
a lot and was more than willing to tell me her story.

"I had an astrocytoma. They are tumors shaped like starfish
with arms that reach out in different directions in the brain. It was

burrowing into this side of my head." Her right hand reached up, claw-like, to the right side of her head.

"We have two young children, and my husband and I decided that the most important thing was for me to survive." Her comment felt strange to me—who wouldn't make survival their first priority?

"So. We decided to try this aggressive, experimental treatment. My husband and I decided to try the treatment because we had two kids, and the most important thing was for me to survive." She said this as if for the first time, looking at me with no indication that she'd just repeated herself.

The treatment was a temporary implant of a radioactive isotope in her brain. For the two days it was implanted she wore a helmet to protect her family when they came to see her.

She explained one result of her brain damage was that she got disoriented easily and could only drive a few places in town, never out of town. That alone horrified me. As we talked, she repeated herself several times, telling me things again and again, as if for the first time.

I came to realize that there are various levels of brain damage. On one level you lose memory, on another level you lose your ability to be aware that you've lost memory. Obviously she had survived, and the isotope had killed the tumor, but not without significant collateral damage.

Like those warnings that scroll across the bottom of your television screen in the Midwest—"warning—warning—tornado-approaching-Rice-County—caution—tornado-approaching," one thought ticker-taped along the edge of my awareness during our conversation: "warning—warning—I-do-not-want-to-become-this-woman—warning—warning—I-will-not-become-this-woman."

How much brain damage does it take before you are no longer yourself? I was shocked to discover that I was unwilling to live life on any terms. There were limits to how far I would go, how much brain damage I would risk, just to stay alive.

∞

In March 1995, my chemotherapy treatments were finally done. The scans of my spine and head showed only one tiny spot in my head. It could have been scar tissue or a small bit of tumor hanging on for dear life. Since doctors were unclear whether the tumor was completely gone, the next step was radiation. But radiating what? And at what dose? It is well documented that radiation kills brain cells. How much radiation and to which part of the brain—those were all variables to consider. But because every body is unique, no hard-and-fast rules could predict a specific outcome. We were at a crossroads: which way do we go, and how far do we go? I needed just enough radiation to do the job, but who knows how much is "just enough"? And who draws the line?

The answer to that question depended on the answer to a previous question, one that could not be answered: is the tumor completely gone? One spot on my brain scan looked suspicious, but as one doctor said, "you've had so much done to you, I wouldn't expect your scans to look normal." Still, even clear scans weren't a guarantee. It takes one million tumor cells before a spot the size of a period appears on a scan. One little tumor cell could be hanging around, twiddling its thumbs, just waiting for its chance to grow. Testing my cerebral spinal fluid was helpful, but not conclusive.

Dr. Neuwelt is almost maniacal in his drive to prevent permanent side effects from brain tumor treatment. I am sure this concern has been the driving force in developing his program. He writes: "One of the goals of enhanced chemotherapy delivery is to delay or eliminate the need for radiation therapy. Although an effective modality for some tumor types, radiation has proven to impact intellectual and cognitive ability. This is a particularly important issue in children."

Greg and I met with Dr. Neuwelt and Dr. Johnson, OHSU's chief radiologist. Dr. Johnson, an older man with nervous little brown eyes, settled in next to Annie. The five of us faced each other around a table in a break room on the radiation floor. The fact that we were actually having this discussion meant that this phase of treatment was different from my treatment to that point. The disruptions were extremely regimented: from when you get phenolbarbital to being given the OK to get out of bed the next day. Your opinion had really no effect on what you would endure.

But radiation was different. We discussed radiation options, from full head/spine irradiation, to a more focused radiation directed at the pineal gland. As we talked about the plusses and minuses of the two plans, Dr. Johnson asked Dr. Neuwelt about a former patient. The man was a neurosurgeon who had worked at OHSU. He was struck with a pinealblastoma and was treated only with cranial/spinal irradiation at the same doses we were considering.

"How is Doctor Brown? Do you know if he's still alive?"

"He's alive. Been out five years now." Dr. Neuwelt said.

"Is he living on his own?"

"No, he can't live on his own. He lives in an assisted living arrangement."

I was instantly afraid. A brain surgeon could no longer live independently as a result of cranial-spinal irradiation. A woman could no longer negotiate complex tasks or participate in a coherent conversation due to radiation-caused brain damage. The images of these two stayed with me, terrifying reminders of what was possible. I knew I did not want to live my life if I could not function on my own. I drew the line.

After much debate, Dr. Neuwelt, Dr. Johnson, Annie, Greg, and I decided to take the conservative route: Protect my cerebral cortex and the verbal centers in my brain by pointing the most powerful radiation at the pineal region.

I felt an uneasy peace. With this strategy my risk of recurrence might be higher, but the risk of brain damage was definitely less. Trading in hearing to survive is one thing. Trading brain cells simply to live—that was a whole different ballgame. I felt like I was bargaining with the devil, debating risks that were entirely unacceptable. But at least the decision was made.

Or so I thought.

Because Greg was teaching a class at Seattle University, we decided to have the radiation treatments at the University of Washington. We packed up boxes of books, and moved in with my parents for two months, the spring of 1995.

At the U., we met with Dr. Karen Lindsley, a national expert on radiation therapy for pediatric brain tumors. We discussed the plan we'd developed with her. Dr. Neuwelt had warned us she probably would not be supportive of a conservative treatment plan, and he was right. While she said she would do what I wanted, she strongly suggested full cranial-spinal irradiation. Looking at my scans, she said that with the aggressive treatment I'd endured and the dramatic response from it, it would be insane to back off now. The fact that she was only theoretically familiar with the Blood Brain Barrier Disruption program made her a bit suspect in my mind. She had no personal experience with it; how could she tell with a few scans what had really happened in my brain? How could she know what she was looking at without a clear understanding of my treatment to that point? I learned later that my initial scans showed the largest and most extensively spread case of a pineal-blastoma she had ever seen.

"But there was this brain surgeon at OHSU who had a pineal and he had full head/spinal irradiation, and he can't live on his own! What's that about?" I pressured her. "I met a woman whose brain was so damaged that she could no longer drive her car out of town—what kind of life is that?"

"Those situations are rare. It's not going to happen to you."

"How do you know? What happens if my brain is so damaged that I am no longer me?" I pleaded. I pushed. I begged. I wanted her to give me scientific certainty that when she sent radiation to kill any renegade tumor cell doing the backstroke in my cerebral spinal fluid, my brain would hold up its end of the deal and come through unscathed.

She shook her head.

"Look, you've been incredibly aggressive with treatment so far. And you have been amazingly successful. If we continue an aggressive treatment, we might just beat this thing. This is no time to back off."

I was amazed at her ability to talk me through this; she literally spent hours with Greg and me, answering the same questions again and again. She admitted I would most likely have some brain damage, but that statistically it would be minimal.

Greg and I talked after; he was not as concerned about side effects as I was. Like a pissed-off bulldog clinging to my heels, my imagination would not relent. Statistics meant little to me; statistically I was not supposed to have gotten this brain tumor in the first place.

I need to come clean here. Even under normal situations, I am not great at making decisions. I like to think it's because I am luxuriously open minded. I credit my terrific imagination with allowing me to see all kinds of possibilities in most things. But there is a backside to an elaborate imagination. Combine it with the awareness that anything can happen—*anything*—and the result can paralyze me. I see pitfalls as well as possibilities in most choices.

On a plane flight I'd taken before my tumor, I watched a travel show about Jamaica. It was terrifically enticing—palm trees, sandy white beaches, people dancing lazily around while sipping from coconuts. At one point, the video showed people jumping off a cliff hundreds of feet high. Each diver hesitated for a split second, then went plummeting down, legs and arms waving wildly, splashing into a deep pool. *Could I do that? Yeah, maybe I could do that . . . Well, maybe.*

Then I remembered what it felt like to jump off the boat-house roof into Lake Washington at my aunt and uncle's place. The hesitation, looking down at my toes hanging over the edge, the flutter of panic like so many butterflies trapped in my gut. Already feeling the humiliation siblings and cousins were sure to heap on me if I wimped out. But remembering too the voice screaming in my head. *DON'T DO IT! What? Are you absolutely nuts? My God! DON'T DO IT!* It's the same voice I must silence every time I'm sitting on a plane waiting for takeoff. *You know, don't you, if this thing goes down, you're toast?* My imagination won't shut up at times like these. It gives me graphic glimpses of what is possible. The plane hasn't yet left the ground, and I'm wondering who might come to my funeral. Where would they hold it? Would they serve nuts after?

The woman in the coffee shop, the former neurosurgeon: my imagination had a heyday with them both. Given that, the decision about my radiation treatment was entirely impossible to make. But I wasn't standing on a cliff or a roof where I could back away. More like a pinnacle. That I jump was a given. The question was, which way?

I decided the only thing to do was to have the experts talk to one another. I arranged a conference call between Dr. Neuwelt, Dr. Johnson, and Dr. Lindsley. Greg and I were still living with my parents, but he was gone, teaching. I was upstairs with the phone in my parents' guestroom. I sat on the edge of the bed while I dialed their numbers. I expected that after listening to them debate treatment options, I would know in my gut which way to jump.

"We have developed a more conservative plan of radiation treatment to minimize the effects of brain damage." Dr. Neuwelt started.

I heard Dr. Johnson make appropriate grunts when Dr. Neuwelt spoke.

"Yes," Dr. Lindsley answered. "I understand your proposal. However, I think it is important to continue a more aggressive treatment to increase the likelihood of a long-term response."

The conversation went back and forth between these two poles. The three doctors politely stuck to their main points, neither view moving closer to the other. After about fifteen minutes I realized the only thing they agreed on was that it was my decision to make. They politely said their goodbyes and hung up.

I protested to the dead phone, "But I can't do this! I can't make this decision! It's so not fair. I don't have time to go to med school and then more time to specialize in brain surgery! How am I supposed to do this?" I heard the dial tone of the phone off the hook, pointlessly beeping, and understood only one thing. There was no right answer. It was finally up to me to make the decision. I had the unbearable freedom to choose. No one was going to do it for me. No one.

I held the receiver to my chest and sobbed. I fell back onto the bed and curled into my knees and cried.

To be honest, I could not imagine that at this most critical point, God would leave me to my own devices. I fully expected that in this conversation someone would say something, if not definitively, then in passing, some word that would catch my heart, hit my gut, send my imagination in one direction. Some kind of intuitive confirmation, not necessarily rational but somehow real nonetheless, that would speak courage to my heart and take the away the fear.

There was no word.

In my younger days when I talked with people about hell, I would describe hell as the absence of God. I would then wisely observe that we on earth were not living in hell, that God was present with us, even if we didn't acknowledge him. It was a way to take seriously the possibility that there was a place where God chose not to be present. It was a way to sound thoughtful and avoid the whole image of hell's flames being tended by some little red-robed, horned man holding a pitchfork and directing traffic, a la Gary Larson.

Sobbing in the dark, the handset of my phone my only comfort, I craved the presence of something. Anything. Anything would have better than the void. I would've taken Gary Larson's hell in a heartbeat. It would have at least given me something definite. I would have had a concrete target to rage against. And in the resistance, I would have known that I was still there. Still vital. Still struggling, however futile the struggle, for life.

But in a void, where is the enemy? I was abandoned to the darkness. In her poem, "On the Cross," Anna Kamienska considers the loneliness Jesus knew on the cross, of dying alone, forsaken even be God. She writes, "All had happened that was to happen between someone and God."[1]

Journal entry:

> I just began reading this book of poems a friend gave and this poem about the crucifixion set something off in me—not sure what—possibly a new way of thinking about it? "Loneliness stood there by his side . . . the mother of all sorrows." An incredible image of being destitute—your only companion is the knowledge that you have none. My God, my God why have you forsaken me?
>
> A view of the cross from Jesus' eyes. Jesus takes on the suffering of abandonment. At that moment, Jesus experiences the utter absence, the silence of no-answer, no word. Surely no embrace. Sudden silence. "All had happened that was to happen between someone and God." He bore our sins, so says the church—but did he bear the unbearable—God forsaking us? I think of how the disciples must've felt forgotten—forsaken.
>
> And I think, too, of my Down syndrome friend, and that evil, evil man who stole her purity and sent her into the suffering of trying to redeem herself. That was evil and that was his choice. But, there is forsakenness, too, isn't there? My God, why did you forsake her? It cuts both ways. Mother Theresa spoke of loneliness as the ultimate human suffering. Did she mean being forsaken, finally by *you*? And I think of the Hebrews' ancient fear of being forgotten, left on some wayside—negated by

---

1. Anna Kamienska, "On the Cross," in *The Gospels in Our Image: An Anthology of Twentieth-Century Poetry Based on Biblical Texts,* ed. David Curzon (New York: Harcourt Brace, 1995) 231.

neglect. Like the man attacked in the Good Samaritan story, the only companion on the road, loneliness, standing at his side.

There is an unlikely hope, then, at the cross. There is the hope that we are finally not alone. As Jesus knew God's absence, Jesus knows even in the darkest of places the anguish of the void. The hell of one forsaken.

After Dr. Lindsley's continued assurances that I would be only mildly affected by radiation, I began to research ways to mitigate brain damage. My friend Hunter knew of a boy who had a pineal-blastoma and had had radiation, and after five years is still alive. I talked with the boy's mother. They had initially tried conventional chemotherapy, with no response. He then had full head/spine irradiation. She described a type of radiation treatment called "hypo-fractionation," which splits the daily dose, giving half in the morning and half in the afternoon. This method is based on data that indicate tumor cells die a bit faster than brain cells when exposed to radiation. If the dosage is split, the hours between radiation exposures give the brain cells a chance to recover faster than tumor cells.

I asked what kind of side effects he had experienced. While she admitted to short-term memory loss and a struggle with math, she assured me they were mild troubles, mitigated with a few tricks to help his memory, and more time on math concepts. Other than that, her son was alive and thriving.

It was an interesting concept. I asked Dr. Lindsley if she was willing to give hypo-fractionation a shot. She agreed. I decided to have full cranial/spinal irradiation using hypo-fractionation.

A full dose of radiation lasts close to one second. Half a dose would last half a second—like a quick beep. But with the traffic going against me as I drove from my parents' home east of Seattle, in Issaquah, with the time waiting and then getting set up in the exact position, each time I went in took me several hours—twice a day—for a half second of radiation. It became my full-time job to go in for treatment. But sitting in traffic and sitting in a doctor's waiting room was nothing compared to a disruption. And it was only for six weeks. I was determined to do what I could to protect my brain.

The radiation was given in the basement of the hospital, but Dr. Lindsley's waiting room was brightly lit and comfortable in its own way. It was clearly a waiting room—with rows of chairs and stacks of magazines—but it had a lived-in feel. It was the children who did it, sitting on the soft-blue carpet, busy, so busy, playing with wooden blocks and plastic toys scattered on the floor. One little girl sat in a corner reading. When children came into the room, they went straight to the spot they had claimed as their own, against the back wall by the big, colorful fish tank. The royal blue and yellow fish swam lazily in their oversized tank, satisfied with their lot in life. Sometimes, a toddler wandered over to check up on them. Only the few abandoned wheelchairs and a bald child here and there indicated this was no ordinary waiting room.

When I came to that room, I liked to watch the little ones play. Usually a sick kid was accompanied by siblings, and they played together on the floor. The drive to play runs strong in kids. It must. How else to explain that even in this room, hidden away from the rest of the world, where nothing is normal, the children seemed as if they were home, playing in their family room. At home. Safe.

This place, with the fish tank and children's giggles, was the core of desperation. I looked at the children playing and at the moms and dads sitting in the chairs, and my heart broke. They sat, waiting for the time when their child's brain would be irradiated to kill the cancer growing in it. Desperation was watching your little one play on the floor and knowing that for her, life, if it will be at all, will never be what it could have been; and there's not a damn thing you can do about it.

Dr. Lindsley regularly came into the waiting room. She would sit down with the children and their parents; she spent whole minutes talking with them, playing with a toy, looking into their eyes. She appeared to be more like the director of a childcare center than a nationally known expert on radiation therapy for pediatric brain tumors. Simply the fact that she would come was a grace. Her calm presence gave me hope.

Still, I felt ashamed watching the children. Was it shame or something else? Hopelessly sad—like watching a boat sink with children on it and being unable to do a thing about it. I was keenly aware that I had had the great fortune of living thirty years before I needed this room. The little ones at my feet—they were just getting started.

There is no way to redeem this.

One spring day four weeks into my radiation treatment, I was driving to the hospital and thinking about my debates with Dr. Lindsley. When she had said, "If you have full head/spine irradiation, I am fairly certain we can beat this thing," it was the first time a doctor had been so bold with me, so confident about me. At this point in treatment, I had experienced few side effects, but Dr. Lindsley made it clear that the side effects of radiation are unpredictable and can show up months, sometimes years, after treatment. As I took the exit off the Evergreen Bridge and rounded the corner toward the University of Washington, I started to think about Easter. *Maybe I'll be around for next Easter. Maybe I'll be able to enjoy several more Easters.* It was the first time I gave myself the permission to peek ahead. A thrill went up and down my spine. I let out a small giggle.

10

⬿⬾

Limping

*. . . they wrestled all night until a gray dawn began to streak
the sky. Jacob's adversary touched him in the hollow of his thigh
and put his thigh out of joint.*[1]

—Walter Wangerin

*Jacob comes away wounded, limping. That reminds us that
encounters with God are very serious experiences, and we
will come away wounded—but believing.*[2]

—John Kselman

BEFORE I finish writing my check, I know there is something
wrong. Things are too still, as if someone has pushed the pause
button on the DVD player. I look up to see I've done it again. The

1. Wangerin, *The Book of God: The Bible as a Novel* (Grand Rapids:
Zondervan, 1996) 67.

2. John Kselman, in *Genesis: A Living Conversation*, ed. Bill Moyers (New
York: Doubleday, 1996) 280.

irritated eyes of the grocery checker, half my age, tell me a question hangs in the air. I understand in her gaze that my answer will set things back in motion. But I rarely come to this store and forget that here, they bag the groceries for you. Glancing down the counter, I see a teenager in an apron, my groceries piled up before him. Clearly put out, he says in his disgusted-with-the-entire-adult-world voice, "paper or plastic?"

I feel the familiar impulse to explain myself, to tell them I'm not the horrible, uncooperative person they take me for. Nor did I come into the store with the evil intent to ignore them and bring their world to a skidding halt. It is simply that I am hearing impaired. It is impossible to answer a question that is not asked.

Hearing impaired. The first few years after treatment, I hesitated to use the phrase. It sounded too politically correct—like calling oneself intellectually challenged. The term set me apart in a self-justifying way that I didn't want or think was necessary.

But the truth is, I did not walk away from the wrestling match unscathed. I am terrifically hearing impaired. In an audiogram, where normal hearing jumps happily along certain points, mine starts out fine with low tones, but as the hearing test raises the pitch of the tones, the line marking my hearing ability takes a nosedive in the middle. High frequency tones no longer exist for me—the line crashes to earth.

To say I am hearing impaired really doesn't say much. It is a general term, running the gamut from a slight hearing loss, where a few high-pitched tones are missed, to a significant loss, where only loud, deep tones are sensed, with no clarity or comprehension. Without my hearing aids, I land closer to the deaf side of that spectrum, with 0 percent speech comprehension in my left ear and 20 percent in my right.

To test the extent of my hearing loss, the audiologist puts me in a soundproof room. I wear headphones. The audiologist says a word in my ear at a normal volume, a two syllable word like *baseball* or *hotdog*. It's my job to guess what word he's saying. He hides his lips so I can't read them and keeps track of my score. In my left ear, I can't guess one word. My right ear gets two out of ten. My top-of-the-line hearing aids help me function in the hearing world. Most of the time. If it's quiet. If I can see your lips. If you speak English without an accent. If your words are neither whispered nor yelled. On the phone I'm a complete disaster. It takes training and a truckload of patience to talk with me. That and a good sense of humor.

I could say it is like trying to have a conversation on the phone when there is a really bad connection: crackles and the hiss of static get in the way, making the words muffled and covered up. Or I could say it is like when you have a really bad cold, and someone is talking to you (you know that because you can see their lips move), but what you can hear of their speaking sounds acres away. I could tell you my impairment is like these things, and it would be true.

And it would be a total lie. Because when you are a hearing person, and then you become a hearing-impaired person, you leave the world as you know it. It is like permanently sitting at the bottom of a pool while someone is standing on the side of the pool saying something to you. You can see their watery image, and some sounds make their way down to the pool's bottom, but those are just sounds. The words are no longer for you.

What I mostly hate is that I have no control. My ability to be involved—be it when I'm at dinner out with friends, or when I'm sitting around a circle in my book club—rests entirely on the thoughtfulness of others. I can do my "speak-this-way-because-I'm-hearing-impaired" speech, but that doesn't mean group members will do it or even care.

Being hearing impaired gives me one way to sense a person's character. They either remember or they don't. Some get it, others don't. Some are unlikely heroes. One is Mark, Catherine's husband. Whenever I visit them, Mark practically shouts to me. I finally told him on my last visit that I loved him for remembering to speak up, but he really didn't need to shout.

Another hero was Dr. Johnson.

Dr. Johnson is a dentist, and he is one of my heroes. To understand the impossibility of that sentence, you have to know one thing: I hate going to the dentist. Going to the dentist falls just below mammograms on the top-ten list of things to avoid. I personally think the urban myth that the field of dentistry has one of the highest suicide rates makes perfect sense. Mucking around in people's mouths on a daily basis for years—in mouths that at that moment are not terrifically grateful for the work you're doing—that's got to have some kind of cumulative negative karma build-up effect. But I'm getting off the track.

Dr. Johnson. Before I left Albany, I had to have quite a bit of dental work done. I decided I wanted a new dentist, when my previous dentist basically called me a wimp for wincing at the no-vocaine needle. I have an unusually stubborn nerve structure in my mouth. Whenever I need novocaine, they might as well truck it in by the gallon; it takes multiple shots to do the trick. So I went on the hunt and found Dr. Johnson.

He didn't make fun of my jaw's nerve structure, so he made points off the bat. But that is not why he is a hero to me. And he wasn't my hero because he was a tall, good-looking blond with perfect teeth and startling blue eyes. Although I confess, those things made going to the dentist a bit more fun! He was a hero because I only needed to tell him once. The first time I sat in his chair and he tilted me back, making small talk, I went into my usual litany about how I'm hearing impaired, blah, blah, blah; and how I needed to see his lips to understand him. He immediately took off his mask; looking up at him, I made some crack about the challenge of lip reading upside-down.

I didn't know he was a hero until my second visit. I sat in the chair; he came up behind me, making small talk. As he talked, he started to turn his back to me to get something off the counter. He wasn't there yet when he remembered, and suddenly his head popped up and he jumped around to face me.

I didn't know a jump could feel like love.

He never forgot and often had to remind his assistants to lower their masks when they talked to me.

I think of him often because he taught me something. He taught me that it's possible for people to remember that I am hearing impaired; it is possible to remember that it takes a certain awareness to talk to me. Dr. Johnson did it, and he was a dentist, for God's sake.

So I have proof that it is possible for the average bear to remember that I don't hear very well. And although to the best of my knowledge there have been no scientific studies to test what percentage of the hearing population pays attention to the Deaf experience, from my deaf experience it would be in the single digits.

If you are reading this carefully, you will notice that when I use the word *deaf*, sometimes I begin it with a capital *D*, and other times I begin it with a lowercase *d*. I use a lowercase *d* when I speak of my own deaf experience. The capital-*D Deaf* refers to an entire subculture: the Deaf community. It is unique unto itself—with its own myths, stories, heroes, jokes and games. And it is a tight community. I use the word *deaf* with a lowercase *d* to refer to my own deaf experience because I am not a member of the Deaf community; I am a member of the hearing culture.

The summer I was taking American Sign Language (ASL) in Berkeley, I did an internship at a Deaf Catholic church in San Francisco. My volunteer job was to welcome people at the door, and if they were visitors, to introduce them to others.

One Sunday I took an older woman downstairs to the coffee hour after the service. I led her to a woman standing close by, but as I was about to sign her name for the visitor, her face lit up with a big smile, and the two of them laughed and hugged.

"What? What?" I signed, confused.

"Two of us? Know. Long ago, long ago we in school same. Together we grow up. Not see each other twenty years!"

It used to be that Deaf children went to boarding schools for their education. It was a way for them to be normal, to make friends with other Deaf kids, and to learn using their native language while furthering their understanding of ASL.

But with the advancing technology of the cochlear implant, an intense debate now rages through the Deaf community. The Deaf vehemently resist the broader culture's attempt to see them as disabled. Further, they treasure their distinct community, and some fear that with implants giving Deaf children the ability to hear, the children will no longer need to learn ASL; they will no longer learn the stories and jokes and games of their Deaf brothers and sisters. Given that 90 percent of Deaf children born to hearing parents know nothing of this rich community life, cochlear implants are seen as a real threat.

My close friends and Greg regularly join me out here on the edge of the hearing/deaf world, and they do a great job. They don't mind that I am now a human, interactive thesaurus on the phone: "I'm not hearing that! Pick a different word!" They rifle through words, come up with a few synonyms, and if things get desperate, start describing things.

"You know, when it's cold outside and you put something on your head to keep yourself warm?"

"Oh, not *cat* or *fat*—but *hat*! I get it." Is this how Dr. Seuss came up with his stories?

At other times we laugh at my bizarre internal life. More times than not, I hear things people did not say. Often, what I hear is more interesting. When one tries to decipher someone else's messy handwriting, the reader's mind tries to find words to fit the shapes of the letters. So my mind scans words to fit the sounds I hear. Because I can't hear high-pitched sounds, it is impossible for me to hear the difference between a *t* sound and a hard *c* sound. You might say "top" and I might hear "cot." I don't do great with middle pitches either, which means vowel sounds aren't to be trusted. A word can be distorted in all kinds of ways. What someone actually says and what my mind hears are often completely different. For the fun of it, I sometimes repeat what I hear: "You want me to water the elephant? I didn't know we had an elephant!"

Besides giving us reasons to laugh, my hearing impaired can be a definite asset in a conflict. The year after my treatments, I worked as a manager for an employment company. As manager I had the privilege of handling all of the angry callers. By the time they reached me, the caller was usually fired up and spewing out all manner of accusations. When they stopped to catch their collective breath, I informed them that I was hearing impaired, and they would need to slow down if they wanted me to hear. Most people were caught off guard, and then the sympathy factor usually kicked in. But even if it didn't, unless you are Hannibal Lecter, it is almost physically impossible to be stark-raving mad and to speak slowly. When they talked slower, their anger usually came down a couple of notches.

There are some advantages to being hearing impaired.

Still, lest I come off as some kind of deaf Pollyanna and you rush out to find your own way to this silent world, let me warn you of the bad news. It is not just my hearing I've lost. I can no longer distinguish sounds. Was that thump in the night a bad thump or just a thump? Smoke alarms go off without a sound. I will be in the middle of a conversation with someone, only to have them get up and walk out of the room midsentence. Even now, sometimes, it isn't until I hear a voice in the other room that I realize they've answered the phone. One great irony of my hearing loss is that I no longer experience honest, true silence. My ears ring constantly; sometimes for the sake of variety, they beep. I miss the quiet. I remember when I really enjoyed music. I miss the rain tapping on my roof. I wish I could hear children when they talk to me.

Deaf or dead? Put that way, what choice is there? I am shocked at my ignorance, remembering the conversation I had early on when

Pam came to stay with me for the "snow" day. We talked about how it wasn't a huge price to pay for my life. I knew not what I was saying.

I've become adept at the daily ways I need to advocate for myself. In any new situation, if I want to participate, I have to teach people how to speak to me: slow down, enunciate, pretend I'm your deaf grandfather. I need to see your lips to hear you. Some people get it, other people don't.

Frankly, there are times when it's just not worth it. There are times when I bag the whole "lessons on speaking to an almost deaf person," opting instead to fake it. I become a viewer watching a silent film. I pay attention to body language. I laugh at an unheard joke. When the mood shifts, I put on my serious face, knit my eyebrows together, and look as if I'm paying attention. To be honest, most of the times I decide to fake it are usually in the context of a larger party, when I am not the sole attendee, and I'm only tangentially connected to begin with. I fake it when I don't know the people well, or when I'm pretty sure I won't be seeing them again. And then there are times I decide to fake it after I've made several requests for the others to speak up, which they do after a quick apology, for a few sentences, then return to their old habits of speaking. These are times when I realize I can say, "What? Come again? Sorry?" until Jesus comes, and things really won't change. I am only willing to interrupt conversations a certain number of times. It slowly dawns on me that they could give a rip, at which point I ask myself why I do.

Sometimes I feel a flicker of guilt, a slight twinge of shame at my own insincerity.

Deaf or dead? The choice isn't really that clear cut. Because there is a kind of death when one has lived a whole life in the world of the hearing, when one's family and friends—her life community —are of the hearing world.

For the most part, my hearing impairment is simply the way it is. Then, usually when I am looking the other way, the stranger comes flying down the riverbank and knocks me down. As I was sitting at church with a nonfunctioning listening assisted device recently, it hit me: I am different than every other person in this room. I finally saw it. I am no longer like the people surrounding me in a fundamental way. I cannot hear. And they can. Which means they participate with one another and the world in a way I do not. Cannot. It doesn't even feel the same as going to a foreign country where the language is entirely incomprehensible to you. There's a good chance if you stay long enough, you'll begin to get it. No chance like that for me. The tears that usually come so readily when I try so hard to hear didn't come that morning. Instead the stone cold hardness of what my life is now. Alone. In a quiet, fundamental way.

At parties people tell jokes I can't hear, and when I ask, "What? What?" the moment is gone, and no one wants to repeat something that is no longer funny. I try hard not to take their frustrated tones of voice and heavy, worn-out sighs personally. But there are moments when I wish they could hear what I don't. I wish they could live a day like me, and understand all of the ways I fight to be a member of the hearing world.

In his book *Genesis*, Bill Moyers is having a conversation with Dr. John Kselman, professor of Old Testament at Weston School of Theology. They're reflecting on the story of Jacob's wounding by the angel:

> *John:* I think it's the text's way of saying that when you encounter God, when you wrestle with God, you're not going to leave that encounter unchanged. And the change can be a hurtful change. Any change or moment of transition in life can be painful because it means leaving something behind and moving forward.

> *Bill:* What does it mean for Israel that as a people, they emerge from a struggle with God?

> *John:* That's the story of this human community of the people of Israel—that their history is a history of a struggle with God, of opposition to God, of being wounded by God in the struggle, and yet of being blessed by God, too. The story encapsulates all of that. Think of what this story must have meant when Israel was in exile in Mesopotamia and in Babylon, as Jacob was. This story would tell them that as our ancestor Jacob met God in the night, so we can still meet God in the long night of our exile.
>
> *Bill:* What's the importance of the wound? Jacob limps away from this wrestling match with a wound that is not just a bruise but a permanent injury. He never forgets it, nor are the people of Israel allowed to forget it.[3]

I can never forget. My hearing impairment is with me when I go to bed at night, there to greet me in the morning. I live on the fence between two worlds. One foot in both, not a member of either.

In one of my ASL classes we were shown videotapes with stories signed by Deaf people. One man signed the story of ordering a burger at McDonald's. In his introduction, he explained that communication is a two-way street. If he takes all of the blame for the communication problem, as if he were somehow broken, then hearing people will look down on him. He began his story describing what he was wearing—a leather coat, bracelets on both wrists, and dark sunglasses. He thought he looked very cool.

He and his Deaf friend went up to the counter at McDonald's; his friend began to write out his order.

"Doing what?" he signed to his friend. "Not need write order. Watch me."

3. John Kselman, in *Genesis: A Living Conversation*, ed. Bill Moyers (New York: Doubleday, 1996), 304–5.

"Want Big Mac . . . French fries," he signed to the teenager behind the counter.

She waved her hands wildly, jumped up and down and ran out. He told his friend, "See? She bring me picture menu will."

While he was bragging to his friend, the girl brought out a menu and put it before him. When he looked down, he saw she was giving him a Braille menu. He whipped off his sunglasses and signed deliberately, "I see you, can!"

His friend wasn't so impressed. Still. I understand it. He refuses to let hearing people look down on him and refuses to take all the responsibility for communication.

I am slowly coming to agree.

When I lived in Minnesota, I had one friend who always exaggerated her lip movements when she spoke with me; she reminded me of a dog that's got peanut butter stuck to the roof of its mouth; you know how they stick out their lips and lick and lick with a confused look, trying to get it off. She did look a little silly, and sometimes she'd forget, and after leaving me she would talk with other friends like that, until they asked, "Mary Sue, why are you talking like that?" Still, I loved her for it. She never forgot. And here, in San Francisco, a soft-spoken friend asks me again and again, "Can you hear me? I want to learn how to talk to you."

I want to come stand beside you and get a glimpse into what life is like for you. I treasure those who choose to come out to the fence and join me.

What breaks my heart is that I no longer look forward to spending time with my family. They are a warm group, funny and active, driven mostly by Steve's terrific sense of humor. They move fast, they talk fast, and at first when I join them, I try my hardest to keep up, hoping against hope that this time will be different. Hope dies slowly when it remembers a different time, a time when I was fully a part of this family. And there are times when someone will look in my direction to say something that is clearly meant for me, but it is just a moment. Brief. And then the real conversation continues.

There was one family vacation wherein the balance shifted, and for a few brief days, I felt fully included.

Mom had just finished her first class in ASL. She worked terrifically hard; it was an excellent class, not only teaching the language, but also teaching about Deaf culture. Before we got together she kept saying she was really looking forward to talking to me.

I kept my expectations low. How much could she learn in one semester?

To my surprise, her vocabulary was terrific, as was her sensitivity toward me. She kept signing to me, "Hear that, you?" or "Think what, you?" or, "Drink what, you?" It felt like the teeter-totter had shifted; I was no longer stuck at the bottom. The balance shifted and I was headed towards the sky.

Unfortunately, that lasted all of one trip. Mom's second ASL class was not nearly as fun, and she realized that it was a lot of work that filled her schedule, limiting travel time for her and Dad. She lost motivation, as she wasn't planning on taking another class. Her signing became sloppy, and she was unfocused.

In an e-mail I tried to explain to Mom why I was less than enthusiastic about getting together with the family:

> I sometimes wish I was totally deaf. Then the family would have to deal with me. Then they could no longer forget that I am not hearing them. I guess the fact that there are times I can hear, and there are times when I'm really good at faking it—something I sometimes do without even realizing it—it gives them permission to not pay attention.
>
> Do you remember the private pool a few blocks down the street from us when we lived in Salem? [It was a small pool, surrounded by some grass and a tall, wood-slatted fence.] I remember swimming in the pool, and occasionally one of the neighborhood kids whose family wasn't a member of the pool would stand outside the fence, peeking through the slats. I always felt sad for him and a little ashamed. I couldn't imagine how awful

it would feel to stand outside the fence on hot summer days and watch other kids having so much fun.

I am now that kid, standing outside the fence.

During baptism, the pastor or priest dips her thumb in the water and makes the sign of the cross on the person's forehead, declaring that she is marked as Christ's own forever. My hearing impairment is my mark. Every day, this wound sets me apart from most of the communities in my life. Like a scar from a deep cut, or a twisted muscle that will not heal, this is the wound I carry from wrestling with God.

The loss of my hearing is something I can never forget.

11

❦

Miracles

THE YEARS immediately following treatment are the most criti- cal for a brain-tumor survivor. If the tumor is going to recur, chances are strongest it will happen in those first years. Each year fol- lowing, the chances of recurrence drop precipitously. I finished treat- ment in July of 1995. At first I had check-up MRIs every six months. As they continued to be clear, they became annual terror events.

In August of 1997, I was not out of the existential, scary woods by any means. Greg and I sat in the exam room of the clinic wait- ing for Dr. Neuwelt to meet with us and tell us the results of the latest scans. He came in and asked if his daughter, who was at the clinic doing research, could join us, which was fine with me. When she came in, he told me my scans looked great. He introduced his daughter, and I gave her the usual speech: "I'm hearing impaired, so I'm not staring at your mouth because you have lettuce stuck- in-your-teeth. I just need to see your lips so I can hear you." Dr. Neuwelt started to laugh.

"I did that! I did that!" he declared, pointing to me, proud of his artistry, as if being made hearing impaired was all the rage, since breast implants had run into problems. Then he asked me how far out I was—not in general; how far out I was from treatment.

"Two and a half years."

"No," he said. "That's not right. Your count starts the day of diagnoses. You were diagnosed, when . . . January of nineteen-ninety-four, right?" There was nothing wrong with his memory.

"Right."

"Then, you're out three and a half years."

"Wow! You just gave me another year!"

Then he said words I will never forget. Remember, Dr. Neuwelt is not a gambling man. You don't want the man to play the stock market with your nickel. He might speak in percentages, but is never one to give false hope.

"At this point, the likelihood of you recurring is pretty slim."

Later, when I saw him in the hallway, he was laughing. "I'm so glad my daughter got to meet you. You're a success story!"

"Why?" I asked. "Haven't you had success with other patients?"

"Oh, yes, of course. But you, you were a long shot. I didn't know if you'd make it. I've never seen such a large pinealblastoma, and one that was so disseminated throughout the spine."

Did I hear him right? Did he just say that? To be told, in this place where for the last several years I'd only been told bad news, or guarded but potentially good news, but never, never strongly hopeful news—to be in this place where most news was something I had to brace myself for and guard my heart against, was unbelievable. To have this man, who rarely laughed with me during the two years we waged war against the tumor, to have this man burst out laughing, was confusing and delightful.

When people found out I was writing a book, they often asked what it's about. I try to explain that it is a kind of spiritual autobiography.

If they know me well, they know it is about my brain tumor, and I explain there are several levels to it. On one level I describe what happened; on another, I ponder some of the questions I had for God.

But what *did* happen? Here I am, into the eleventh chapter, and I don't know, finally, what to say. Was it a miracle? Was it luck—simply a matter of timing and coincidence? Or was it synchronicity: things coming together in a weird, unexplained but somehow intentional way?

Many friends and family members are quick to declare me a miracle. But what do they mean by that?

The year I worked for the employment agency, a man I did not recognize came to visit one day. I invited him into my office, and when we sat down, he handed me a book.

He told me there was a letter inside for me.

> Julie,
>
> A few years ago loss was a too familiar part of my life. Divorce, a friend became a quad in a wreck, the talons of cancer grasped Nellie right across the street from me. On and on, one after another. Some folks were close, some were just special to our community.
>
> In finding my own heart I heard you preach several times. You were insightful and had good theology. Then I heard your story. You were special, many shared prayers for you—I wrote you a note back then too.
>
> To shorten a long story . . . I have to add that along life's journey I picked up the habit that I should never meet a person or visit a friend without giving a gift. Usually a bit more simple, but remember you are special. You survived my prayer request and you are the only one who did. I don't pat myself on the back for you being here, but as I said I'm glad you're around. You have moved up the special list on account of you are still here.
>
> In addition to my gift-giving habit, I am also a recovering reader of self-help books. It was an addiction; I read hundreds of them but they never took. This one

caught my eye. Like a good sermon the stories are insightful, they touch my heart. I don't regret the diversion from recovery.

I ordered a new copy special for the occasion of meeting you. I am really having to work on being a gracious receiver. Intellectually I understand it to be as important as giving. Nor do I mean to be preaching, I would be flustered if a stranger gave me a gift. I'm working on not feeling that way, part of my healing. See—in my former self I would have never called and said hi, I'm glad you're alive. But I am, it's special and I hope you can accept this book as an acknowledgment and celebration of that fact. God and I once had a serious, mean, nasty and intense conversation about you and this cancer thing. Reckon the adjectives belong to me not God. I can't say that I won, but this is my way of closing this story and thanking God too.

Dr. Remen makes a lot better sense of life than I do. I hope you enjoy the book.

God Bless,

Dick C.

The book was *Kitchen Table Wisdom: Stories That Heal*, by Dr. Rachel Naomi Remen.

"You are special. You survived my prayer request and you are the only one who did."

The question begs for an answer: was my healing a miracle? Am I here because enough people joined Dick in having it out with God? Did God step in to interrupt natural processes, or step in to direct me to Dr. Neuwelt's program? If so, what does that imply?

I'm uncomfortable with potential conclusions. It puts a lot of pressure on God. Prosecuting Attorney to God: "if it's true that you choose to heal person A, and leave person B to their doom, on what basis, sir, do you make that decision?" It also puts a lot of pressure on me. "You're a miracle! God saved you for a purpose! Now, get to it!"

Still, I *was* at the right place at the right time. If not for my church job in Albany, I most likely would've been across the country from Dr. Neuwelt, living in New Jersey, three thousand miles from the only Blood Brain Barrier program. Chances are great I might never have connected with the program.

In *Telling Secrets*, Frederick Buechner talks about the terrible secret of his daughter's battle with eating disorders. He describes how lost and alone he was during that time.

> I remember sitting parked by the roadside once, terribly depressed and afraid about my daughter's illness and what was going on in our family, when out of nowhere a car came along down the highway with a license plate that bore on it the one word out of all the words in the dictionary that I needed most to see exactly then. The word was TRUST. What do you call a moment like that? Something to laugh off as a kind of joke life plays on us every once in a while? The word of God? I am willing to believe that maybe it was something of both, but for me it was an epiphany. The owner turned out to be, as I'd suspected, a trust officer in a bank, and not long ago, having read an account I wrote of the incident somewhere, he found out where I lived and one afternoon brought me the license plate itself, which sits propped up on a bookshelf in my house to this day. It is rusty around the edges and a little battered, and it is also as holy a relic as I have ever seen.[1]

Buechner was given what he needed most when he needed it. Am I alive now, writing this now, because of a miracle? I don't know. I only know that people across the country prayed for me. I know, too, that many people decided to travel the way with me. I know that I stumbled onto a hugely successful brain-tumor treatment program. This much is true: I was given what I needed at the time I needed it.

1. Frederick Buechner, *Telling Secrets: A Memoir* (New York: HarperCollins, 1991), 49–50.

There it is: the passive voice. Use it often and it is the death knell for any writer. But this time, I can find no other way, no other true way, to say it. *I was given.* I was given what I needed when I needed it. Like the first time. The first time I was given a life, given my life, apart from my intent or will, given it from a power completely outside myself. It is human nature to forget this, I think. We so easily slip from the awareness that we didn't orchestrate our existence into some sense that we are owed. Owed fairness. Owed justice.

And I think of Job, rightly taking God on for the hell his life became. Refusing to accept the responsibility for his suffering, but instead, declaring to God that this life was not fair. And while the story of Job lifts him up as a model of faith, it is hard to forget how God responds to him.

Out of the whirlwind:

> Where were you when I laid the foundation of the earth?
> Tell me, if you have understanding. Who determined
> its measurements—surely you know! On what were its
> bases sunk, or who laid its cornerstone, when the morn-
> ing stars sang together and all the sons of God shouted
> for joy? —from Job 38

God's questions pound Job for two long chapters, just to make sure Job gets the point. God is beyond our limited definitions. God is the one who created life for the pure joy of it. Defending it at times, while at other times letting death have the final say.

I was newly finished with my treatment when I went to hear New Testament scholar Marcus Borg talk about his book *Meeting Jesus Again for the First Time*. It is based on the work of the Jesus Seminar, a group of scholars who've met in attempts to sift through the Gospels, using a set of criteria to distinguish the actual words of Jesus from the words attributed to Jesus by the early church's gospel writers.

In his book, Borg makes a distinction between the pre-Easter Jesus and the post-Easter Jesus. The pre-Easter Jesus is the flesh-and-blood man who lived in Palestine, walked, ate, taught, healed people, and died. The post-Easter Jesus is the Risen Christ, experienced by his disciples after his death. The post-Easter Jesus is the one experienced by the modern church.

In *Meeting Jesus Again for the First Time*, Borg writes, "[Jesus] was a remarkable healer: more healing stories are told about him than about anybody else in the Jewish tradition."[2] In his lecture, speaking of the pre-Easter Jesus Borg affirms that the evidence and nature of the healing stories strongly support a conclusion that Jesus actually did heal people. Yet when Borg moved into his description of the post-Easter Jesus, he made no mention of Jesus Christ as one who heals.

When he took questions at the end, I asked, "You mentioned the pre-Easter Jesus healed people. Do you think the post-Easter Jesus also heals?" What was I looking for? An answer for the past two years of my life? An explanation for what happened? Assurance that it would not come back?

Borg paused, cleared his throat.

"Yes, I believe the post-Easter Jesus heals. I've heard too many unexplained stories of healings to come to any other conclusion. Although I am uncomfortable with the implications of this. It raises all kinds of questions about God's justice. These are questions that I have no answers to."

Marcus Borg is a man who makes his living attempting to demystify the person of Jesus Christ. Borg uses a rational, analytic process to arrive at his conclusions. This man agrees that even in our modern age, Jesus Christ heals us, sometimes physically. As he did on occasion when he was among us.

But I've heard stories myself. Stories where the post-Easter Jesus did not physically heal someone, pray as they might. Too, in the New Testament, Jesus didn't heal everyone. He didn't wave

2. Marcus Borg *Meeting Jesus Again for the First Time: The Historical Jesus and the Heart of Contemporary Faith* (San Francisco: HarperSanFrancisco, 1994) 31.

some God-blessed wand to effect a general healing; nor did those who were sick get better simply by being near him, as if he shed an aura filled with antioxidants and antibacterial cleansers. And there is Mark's disturbing story of the Syrophoenician woman, also found in Matthew, in which she has a theological sparring match to convince Jesus to heal her daughter.

To make matters more complex, the gospels sometimes make a distinction between being "healed" and being "made well." For instance, one woman is healed by touching the hem of Jesus's robe, only to be told later that her confession makes her well. The Greek usage in these stories indicates a distinction between the two. To be "healed" refers to being cured of one's disease. To be "made well" has the idea of rescue from impending destruction, being pulled back from the brink.

I think back to a similar distinction Madeleine L'Engle made the summer of my tumor during my weeklong writing seminar with her. I knew her thoughts on healing came from her own experiences, one of which was the loss of her husband to cancer. That summer I wanted to be told that we can be cured. Physically healed. I wanted someone with authority to tell me it was, indeed, possible. God can make us well in our bodies as well as in our hearts. God had the power to make me well in my flesh, in my bones and in my head. With the future of my life up for grabs, I had little interest in being healed if in the end the tumor won. Madeleine talked about her husband, Hugh's, illness. When he was sick and people asked her how to pray for him, she told them, "Pray for what's best for Hugh." Then she told us, "We can always be healed. Not always cured, but always healed. Healing is deeper and has more to do with love." She too joins the gospel writers in making the distinction between body and spirit.

Is it true, then, that physical healing is less important than being cured? I fear I'm getting too close to the heresy of Docetism, a splitting of the body from the spirit, as if only the spirit matters. Dare I forget Nicholas Wolterstorff's strong conviction that God is a God of life? And if God is a God of life; this God hates anything that is a threat to life.

So what happened to me? I am unable to explain it, and from that arrive at an indisputable claim concerning God's nature. I do know that those whom the pre-Easter Jesus healed asked for their healing. The Syrophoenician woman, the bleeding woman who sneaked up on Jesus, Jairus pleading for his daughter. In whatever way they could find, they asked. Some with a deep conviction, others without any other option. They came to him with a hope that they might get his attention, and with that, be healed. They asked. I do know that. They asked.

God may already know what we need or think we need, but I suspect something happens in the asking. Something happens when we speak out, dare to hope. Name our fears. Putting voice to them, speaking the word, does, I think, change things. So, I bring my prayers—sometimes again and again—like the woman banging on the householder's door in the middle of the night, until finally the door opens a crack and the cranky, sleepy householder with the messed-up hair, sticks his head out if only to stop the racket. "What? What? Can't a guy get a little sleep around here?"

Sometimes I bang on that door until my knuckles are bruised and bloody. Often, I bring it to God because I've nowhere else to go, having exhausted all other possibilities. If God decides to not get involved, and I lose, then the two of us have words.

I can only say what it has been like for me. Again with the passive voice. But the utterly true, no-holds-barred passive voice. I was given a life, and then given it again. By a powerful other who somehow thought the party wouldn't be complete without me.

12

≪•≫

Going Home

COMING BACK to Albany after my radiation treatments was terribly difficult, for there was little to come back to. Greg and I
had our home, but I had no job. Greg was offered a one-year teaching contract at a private liberal-arts school in Minnesota, and given
that he was finished with his dissertation and desperate for work, we
decided he should jump at the chance. We would have a commuter
marriage for nine months. It was not a great situation, but we promised to see each other about every two or three weeks.

I attended the Presbyterian church in Corvallis, a fifteen-min-
ute drive southwest of Albany. As I checked out the want ads, it was
tough to figure how I fit in the secular world. I applied for any non-
profit job opening, without a bite. Frankly, I really don't know how it
happened, but I landed a job as the branch manager of a temporary
employment company. Professionally, I went from a world of sermon writing and hospital visiting to a world of payroll, employment
law, billing practices, and profit reports.

It lasted a year. Greg came back, then was offered a two-year position at different school in Minnesota. We sold our house and moved to Northfield in 1997.

It was there that another miracle happened.

While I lived in Albany, I had avoided downtown, where the church building was. Then after I'd moved away, I could not drive by the town on I-5 without crying. Rather than time healing all wounds, time seemed to cause festering in this wound. Jim, our counselor throughout the tumor, once said that of the two primary events in my life, the tumor and the church closing my position, he thought the latter was more traumatic. He was right. I was completely traumatized by their rejection of me. And even though, after I moved away, the new co-pastors at the church sent me an occasional note, I could not respond to their attempts to make contact.

Then one morning, sitting in our reading chair in our small library in Minnesota, as I sipped my tea and wrote in my journal, for some reason I began to think about the Albany church. I was meditating on the relationship of pain, years of pain that I still carried. It was a long-distance embrace of deep pain on my part and, I assumed, guilt on theirs. My first thought was, as it had always been, I can't forgive them. I simply can't. How do you ignore pain and say that everything is fine? Don't worry about it? Everything was not fine. It was not possible simply to decide to forgive them.

Then my Buddhist friend Steve came into my head and joined the debate. Or better put, I thought of what we'd talked about, how Steve insisted that one thing true of all life was suffering. I knew what he meant. If you cling to something, or love something, you will end up suffering.

So I looked deep into the pain. I realized it hurt so because there was a time when I loved the people at the church. When I was with them celebrating births, performing weddings, sitting beside their hospital beds and praying with them in times of loss, our lives got tangled up together. The people at that church weren't "congregants" in some generic sense. They were Clarissa, stern in her love and strong in her convictions; Angie, gentle and strong;

Jim, quiet and loyal. I knew their stories and why they were who they were. They mattered. To God, surely, but also to me. I realized if I had not cared for them, their decision to end my job would not have hurt so. So I looked at the pain differently, not as something to be avoided or shunned, but as a witness to love. I was hurting deeply because there was a time when I loved them deeply. If so, how can pain be a bad thing? Instead of pushing it away, I invited it in. *Come on in; take a load off; can I get you something to drink?*

Instantly, and I do mean at once, in the next breath, at that precise moment, the pain vanished. I was set free.

During the years following my treatments, Pam continued to work at the church in Albany. Her knowledge and long-held relationships with the people of the church were, I'm sure, things that held the community together in the awkward years that followed my dismissal. At the same time, our friendship continued and deepened. We got together annually for a few days just to talk and stay connected. The life of the church was always a bit of a sticky topic; she knew the pain I felt.

In the spring of 2002, we were in a Portland hotel room, our feet up, glasses of wine in our hands. The sun was low on the horizon, lighting up the sky with a brilliant pink-orange light. The topic of the Albany church came up, and I quietly said that I thought it would be fun to visit the church sometime and worship there.

Pam sat in stunned silence, her face lit up by the lively sky.

"What did you say?"

I told her of my experience in my reading chair and said again, "I think it would be fun to go back."

"Are you interested in preaching?"

That was something I never thought would happen, but the thought delighted me.

"Yes! I would love to preach!"

∞

As they say, timing is everything. The church was in the midst of planning its 150th anniversary celebration. It was to be quite the party, with a full sit-down dinner that evening.

The following are the biblical texts and sermon I preached on the 150th anniversary of the church.

Genesis chapters 17 and 18, selected:

> When Abram was ninety-nine years old the Lord appeared to Abram, and said to him, "I am God Almighty; walk before me, and be blameless. And I will make my covenant between me and you, and will multiply you exceedingly.
>
> And the Lord appeared to Abraham as he sat at the door of his tent in the heat of the day. Abraham lifted his eyes and looked, and behold, three men stood in front of him. When he saw them, he ran from the tent door to meet them, and bowed himself to the earth. They said to him, "Where is Sarah your wife?" and he said, "She is in the tent." The Lord said, "I will surely return to you in the spring, and Sarah your wife will have a son." And Sarah was listening at the tent door behind him. Now Abraham and Sarah were old, advanced in age; it had ceased to be with Sarah after the manner of women. So Sarah laughed to herself, saying, "After I have grown old, and my husband is old, shall I have pleasure?" The Lord said to Abraham, "Why did Sarah laugh . . . and say, 'shall I indeed bear a child, now that I am old?' Is anything too hard for the Lord?" (RSV)

Luke chapter 1, selected:

> The angel Gabriel was sent to a girl betrothed to a man named Joseph, and said to her, "Do not be afraid, Mary, for you have found favor with God. And behold, you will conceive in your womb and you will bear a son, and you shall call his name Jesus. And Mary said to the angel, "How shall this be, since I have no husband?"

Behold, the angel Gabriel replied: "With God, nothing is impossible." (RSV)

"HOW CAN THIS BE?"

Sermon by Julie Anderson Love

OCTOBER 19, 2003

United Presbyterian Church of Albany

> The place to start is with a woman laughing. She is an old woman, and, after a lifetime in the desert, her face is cracked and rutted like a six-month drought . . . She is laughing because she is pushing ninety-one hard and has just been told she is going to have a baby.

So begins Frederick Buechner's account of this Genesis story. He continues:

> The old woman's name is Sarah, of course, and the old man's name is Abraham, and they are laughing at the idea of a baby's being born in the geriatric ward and Medicare's picking up the tab.[1]

Or as Genesis puts it: Between chuckles, Sarah says, "shall I indeed bear a child, when I am so old?" It was utterly absurd to her; how could this be?

Buechner's right to imagine the characters in this comedy cracking up, isn't he? It's even better if you know the story of Abraham and Sarah. It started out with an old promise sealed with a sandy beach and starry sky: Your descendents, like stars and grains of sand, will be too many to count. But the cradle remained empty; their lives quiet. They began to wonder if maybe God needed some help and went about trying to make the promise happen on their own. Who could blame them for trying to nudge fate along? But their attempts failed, tragically so. Then, when the stars had all but

---

1. Frederick Buechner, *Telling the Truth: The Gospel as Tragedy, Comedy, and Fairy Tale* (San Francisco: Harper & Row, 1977) 49.

faded from view, the angel shows up, with unbelievable, absurd news. How can you not imagine a mischievous sparkle in the corner of God's eye? It's impossible to keep a straight face—having a baby at 91? How can this be?

It was the same question Mary asked.

Here she was, one step away from marriage. A young girl, just starting out. But then, with an angel's visit, her life is disrupted by unbelievable, utterly unexpected news. Can you imagine the shock? Not unlike that of her ancestor Sarah! Imagine her surprise. The angel is doing everything she can to keep Mary calm, help her hear this absurd news. And it's hard not to see the angel catching her breath, waiting for Mary to respond. Will she do it? Become a mother before a bride? Take on the burden of this God-child, she who is still more child than woman herself? Thank God Mary had enough wits about her to ask the question, "how can this be?"

It is the question I asked myself last fall. Some of you know, many of you don't, that in January of 1994, I was diagnosed with an extremely malignant brain tumor. It was large, in the center of my head and dispersed throughout my spine. The good news: I survived. Not unscathed, however. Side effects of the intensive chemo treatments, beyond hearing impairment, included the strong likelihood that I was infertile. And so, my husband, Greg, and I lived with that assumption for nine years.

Imagine my surprise to find out I was pregnant! After I took the first pregnancy test, and saw that it was positive, Greg, ever the rational one, said, "O.K., tomorrow, buy a test from a different manufacturer. If that's positive, we'll go to the doctor." I knew what he was doing: hedging his bets. It was too unbelievable to be true. I understood that. We had both lived with the strong assurance that pregnancy for me was not an option. It was seared into our consciousness. So much so that I spent most of my pregnancy waiting for the time when I could finally get my head around the fact that a baby, who wasn't supposed to come, was coming anyway.

Even now, there are moments when I look at her and ask, "Where did you come from?" And to be honest, she has yet to come up with a good answer. I'm not sure she ever will; the question doesn't seem to concern her at all. She looks at me with her deep blue eyes as if to say, "I'm here. Where'd you think I'd be?" And so, I join Mary and Sarah: How can this be?

God's answer to Sarah was, "is anything too difficult for the Lord?" Gabriel's answer to Mary was much the same, "nothing will be impossible with God."

Nothing is impossible with God. Reading this, I initially wanted to turn it around—simply flip this awkward, double negative of a statement into its cheery counterpart: With God, everything is possible. Put a Norman Vincent Peale spin on it. With God, all things are possible. It sounds much better, doesn't it? With God, all things are possible. Anything can happen, one only need ask. The world is really, finally, orderly. A sweet world of light and promises, where God is always right, and God always wins. No need to worry.

So why not put a positive spin on it? After all, the two examples are basically saying the same thing. One is in the negative, the other positive. But then a colleague told me of preacher Rick Spalding, who rightly points out the literal translation: All things are not impossible with God.

"Be not afraid. For with God, all things are not impossible."

With God, all things are not impossible.

Spalding contemplates how he likes the two little parts of speech: "not" and "im" right next to each other where they can have their elemental clash and, perhaps, work that odd alchemy that has mystified me ever since arithmetic: making a positivity out of two negatives.

He goes on to say it's important to start with the negative because that's often where we start.

He's right, you know. Impossibilities surround us—the impossibilities of peace in our ripped-apart world, the impossibility of reconciliation in broken relationships that are crippled by years of misunderstanding and disrespect. Or the past, with its own regrets that can no longer be different, but still linger on the edges of our days, haunting us. Impossible. Impossible to change these things, to make what is broken whole.

So, let us begin with the bad news. Because if what we say as a church, as individuals, about God, has any integrity at all, we have to begin with the reality that is our lives. As much as we hate to admit it, our lives are filled with impossibilities. With the negatives of broken hearts and love torn asunder. And it's not just the brokenness in us, but also the things that come our way, unbidden. We are tossed about in the "pitiless storm" and to deny it would be to lie. So, use the negative, Luke. Use the negative, Gabriel. Let us know you know what you're talking about.

It's only then that the word has power: God's great "NO" to our impossibilities. For God nothing is impossible. Negative crashing against negative to turn things around. God's profound NO! to the negatives in our lives. NO. God refuses to let the impossibilities in our lives have the final say. Be the end of the story. God refuses to have our negatives cripple us with despair.

Be not afraid, for with God nothing is impossible.

Preacher Fred Craddock calls this verse, "the creed behind all other creeds," adding, "The church should recite it often, not only at the manger, not only at the empty tomb, but on any occasion of reflecting on its own life, joy, and hope."[2]

It is a terrific word of hope in our world of bad news upon bad news.

Mary, have a baby? Not impossible.

Survive a malignant brain tumor? Not impossible.

Peace between Israel and Palestine? Not impossible.

---

2. Fred B. Craddock, *Luke*, Interpretation (Louisville: John Knox, 1990) 28.

Would that I could end here, with this word of unbelievable, how-can-this-be news. But there is something else hidden in the two texts that we read this morning.

Buechner hints at it, when he writes of Sarah and Abraham, and even God, laughing at the absurdity of it all:

> One account says that Abraham laughed until he fell on his face, and the other account says that Sarah was the one who did it. She was hiding behind the door of their tent when the angel spoke, and it was her laughter that got them all going. [As Genesis tells it] God intervened then and asked about Sarah's laughter, and Sarah was scared stiff and denied the whole thing. Then God said, "No, but you did laugh," and of course God was right. Maybe the most interesting part of it all was that far from getting angry at them for laughing, God told them that when the baby was born his name should be Isaac, which in Hebrew means laughter. So you can see that God not only tolerated their laughter but blessed it and in a sense joined in it, which makes it a very special laughter indeed—God and [humans] laughing together, sharing a glorious joke in which both of them are involved.[3]

Consider, too, the Lukan story of Mary.

Here she is, contemplating her new life as a married woman. And it is interrupted by unbelievable news. Thank God she had enough wits about her to ask, how can this be? She knew enough about human biology to know what he announced wasn't possible, was, in fact, entirely impossible. After going off the subject a bit—was he buying time, trying to figure out how to explain the workings of the eternal to a woman bound by time?—he finally gets to it: With God, nothing is impossible. To which, her reply, a reply sung throughout the centuries hence, "Here I am, the servant of the Lord; let it be with me according to your word."

3. Buechner, *Telling the Truth*, 52–53.

When Greg and I were in Italy last summer, I couldn't help but notice the plethora of Madonnas—they were everywhere, large and small. There was even a tiny one in a small, carved out space in the side of a brick wall behind our little hotel. Someone kept fresh flowers there, an unlikely altar that shared the alley with a dumpster. Mary is worshipped as the mother of Christ, and no doubt her compliance to this Angel's announcement is just the first step in her exemplary faith. She is adored for her quiet willingness to allow her life to be entirely interrupted. "Behold, I am a slave to the Lord."

As New Testament scholar Jane Schaberg put it: "Mary's saying she is a 'slave' of the Lord is the text most responsible for the impression of her as a passive character, the antithesis of a liberated woman. Is this Luke's way of setting her up as the model for submissive female behavior and of articulating an acceptance of patriarchal belief in female inferiority, dependence and helplessness?"[4]

But surely Mary knew something of what was in store for her. I've no doubt Mary had seen enough pregnancies up close, witnessed births and the deaths some of them caused. Mary knew what it meant.

And she must've known, too, that this would not necessarily be welcome news to the community in which she lived. It took great courage to welcome this Angel-word. Great courage to put her reputation on the line, risk ostracism from family, her betrothed and the only life she knew.

And contrary to how the image in Luke has been interpreted throughout the centuries to idealize the passivity of women, Jane Schaberg suggests an alternative interpretation: "The word slave must be seen in connection with Jewish use of it as an honorary title. "Slave of God" was applied to a few outstanding men of Israelite history (Moses, Joshua, Abraham, David, Isaac, the prophets, Jacob)

---

4. Jane Shaberg, "Luke," in *The Women's Bible Commentary*, ed. Carol Newsom and Sharon Ringe (Louisville: Westminster John Knox, 1992) 284.

and to one woman (Hannah). Luke surely intends the term to have a positive value here."[5]

"Behold, I am God's handmaiden." In response to this startling news, Mary places herself in the company of a most impressive group. "Let it be as you have told me." Clearly, God did not force this new thing upon her; she had a choice. As, I think, did Sarah. The joke they shared, the laughter they shared, God and humanity, is an image of the divine-human partnership in this life we live.

I thought about my own story. For eight years, Greg and I believed we could not get pregnant. And we acted on that assumption, which proved true. And to be honest, infertility was a relief. I wasn't really sure I wanted a child. But in the spring of 1992, a good friend of mine wondered what it would mean for me to get pregnant. She began to spin out the timing of it all. And it didn't bother her one bit that my doctors suggested the strong likelihood that it would not happen. I listened, and a good part of me thought she was entirely off her rocker. Even so, I felt a little twinge of hope, and heard the creak of a door opening slightly. I let myself peek around it. For just a bit, I put aside assumptions about the way things were and imagined what might be.

God is not one to force us into something against our will. We have a choice. If it's only a choice to imagine our impossibilities transformed. That is a choice. That is a decision to imagine our lives beyond their impossibilities. To think, what if? What if this relationship that has been entrenched in bitterness and pain for years were somehow different? What if we were truly able to live in peace with the loss of a loved one? What if we could somehow find peace with God, who hasn't seemed to notice the trouble life's thrown our way? What if I was somehow able to let go of the regrets of my past, set free from self-loathing?

It's a scary proposition, this imagining. Scary because if you can imagine it, it might just happen. And then you no longer have

5. Ibid.

the luxury to nurse that age-old grudge. You can no longer play the victim and continue to self-righteously spin your psychic wheels in the mud. It's a scary proposition because what you are doing is imagining your heart changing. Imagining God saying "No" to the impossibilities in your heart and life.

How can this be?

With God, nothing is impossible.

Amen.